# Southern Scrumptious Entertains

BY BETTY SIMS

*For my family who has always been
in my heart and my kitchen.*

*Southern Scrumptious Entertains*

Published by Scrumptious, Inc.

Copyright © 2002 Betty Brandon Sims
4107 Indian Hills Road
Decatur, Alabama 35603
256-353-1897
mettysims@aol.com
www.scrumptiousinc.com

Library of Congress Catalog Number: 2002102905
ISBN: 0-9659053-1-4

Edited, Designed, and Manufactured by
Favorite Recipes® Press
an imprint of

**FRP**

P.O. Box 305142
Nashville, Tennessee 37230
800-358-0560

Project Manager: Tanis Westbrook
Designer: David Malone
Art Director: Steve Newman

Manufactured in the United States of America
First Printing: 2002
15,000 copies

# Acknowledgments

To my loves, my children, my grandchildren, and Bill, my husband.
Thank you for the love, support, and good times that you have given me
and the courage with which you have faced life under many adversities,
always with smiles, laughter, and hope for the future.

## Artists

### Cover Illustration: Mitch Howell Coon

Mitch is a cover designer and illustrator from Hartselle, Alabama.
She is primarily a watercolor portraitist, but has done a number of book
covers and illustrations. Mitch, a Fine Arts graduate of Birmingham
Southern College, has work represented in collections throughout this
country and abroad. She is listed in the *Who's Who in Art and Antiques*
and is a member of the Watercolor Society of Alabama.

### Line Drawings: Libby Sims Patrick, IIDA

Libby is an award-winning Interior Designer who loves to draw. Her firm,
Sims Patrick Studio, Inc., specializes in commercial and residential
projects. She is my oldest daughter and lives with her husband, Carl, and
their son, Alex, in Atlanta, Georgia.

# Contents

# Southern Scrumptious Entertains

Entertaining our families and friends in our homes continues to gain in popularity. People entertain more formally in the East, according to a recent survey, and more casually in the South. No matter the style of entertaining, everyone wants it to be easy. It also was determined in a recent poll that 87 percent of people worried most about selecting a menu for their guests—what goes with what and other decisions. In *Southern Scrumptious Entertains*, I have given you 25 menus to choose from and directions for doing these easily.

Yes, we have done much entertaining at the Sims, both before owning Johnston Street Cafe and after. For those ten years starting in 1986 at Johnston Street Cafe, we catered myriads of parties, mall openings, wedding receptions, engagement parties, bridesmaids' luncheons, picnics, barbecues, and tea parties.

Actually, when I opened Johnston Street Cafe, I had not intended to cater, but there was a need. People kept calling and insisting that we cater. We began by having people bring their platters by, we would fill them, and they would pick them up. The first wedding that we catered was Patti Pryor's wedding reception at Flower Hill, the lovely home of her parents, Betty and Luke Pryor.

*Southern Scrumptious Entertains* came about as a direct result of many cooking classes at Scrumptious Culinary School—plus a lot of travel, experiencing foods all over the world. I have always enjoyed teaching and began in earnest while I owned Johnston Street Cafe. After selling Johnston Street Cafe in 1998, I immediately began plans for a commercial kitchen designed by Scott Schoels, an outstanding young architect here in Decatur, in the lower level of our home. My husband, Bill, said, "You're going to do what?" This kitchen began my new endeavor of teaching classes at home. I also travel quite a bit, teaching in other places. For the last four years there have been many classes and lots of memories.

What a thrill to use my longtime artist friend, Mitchie Howell Coon, to create the watercolor for the cover and my daughter, Libby, to illustrate with line drawings throughout the book. Daughter Lisa illustrated the first book *Southern Scrumptious*. Sheri, our second daughter, is masterminding the marketing of the book and son Bill is advising me on website information. Entertaining is about "lifting one's spirits," so come along . . . and enjoy these menus for casual occasions and those special "To Dos" and "Tah Dahs."

# Breakfasts & Brunches

# *Menus*

*Festive Family Breakfast*

*An Island Breakfast*

*Home for the Holidays Brunch*

*New Orleans Brunch*

*An Elegant Brunch*

*A Casual Brunch for Friends*

*A Southern Brunch*

This is truly one of my favorite ways to entertain. There is an old saying, "Breakfast like a king, lunch like a prince, and dine like a pauper." This makes sense in terms of good health—our smallest meal at night, the "farmer's way." What could give us a better start to our day than a satisfying meal of breakfast or brunch? My family loves breakfast. We generally have juices, "Metty's pancakes" (a favorite with the grandchildren) or waffles, French toast, or one of the casseroles included. Occasionally, we have eggs benedict, some wonderful fruit concoction, and cheese grits. Brunch is at a later, more sociable, hour than breakfast so it lends itself as a great meal for entertaining friends.

Simple ideas can make a breakfast or brunch special. Fruit in a bowl or basket makes a super centerpiece. Magnolia leaves, my favorite, placed on the table, or five small individual crystal vases with one bloom and a bit of greenery in each, are so easy, but effective. Set the table with your favorite glassware, china, and cutlery, which can range from colorful paper plates to your best crystal, porcelain, and silver. I love a breakfast or brunch buffet. For order of placement, first comes juice, then fruit, main dish, side dishes, breads or coffee cake. Your buffet may be offered in the kitchen, breakfast room, or dining room. Do as much preparation ahead as possible.

Recently, I did a brunch cooking class at Neiman Marcus in Atlanta with the proceeds donated to the Susan G. Komen Foundation. I featured the Italian Strata, since it is a very healthful dish. My girls were present, and I was able to introduce all three, Libby, Sheri, and Lisa. Our family has been touched by breast cancer. We must all do all we can to eradicate it.

Brunch has become an occasion. It is held usually at the most relaxed time of the week, which many associate with comfort, and it epitomizes entertaining in its most casual form. Have fun.

# Festive Family Breakfast

*Apple Juice • Orange Juice*
*Sausage and Egg Casserole with Salsa*
*Orange Butter • Metty's Pancakes*
*Honeydew, Cantaloupe, Raspberries and Cream*
*Honey Nut Granola • Bacon*

This Family Breakfast is very typical of the food the Sims family enjoys when everyone assembles at Sunshine, our home. The grandchildren beg for pancakes every time they visit and want them every morning they are with us. They want huge heart-shaped pancakes that I pour out on the large griddle. These are easy to stir up just before cooking them. The children have a contest to see who can eat the most, so I usually have a bowl of fruit as a centerpiece surrounded by all shapes and sizes of pigs from my collection. Bill, my husband, has carved most of them. The Orange Butter and the granola can be done several days ahead. The Sausage and Egg Casserole, I mix up the night before as well as cutting the fruit and making the cream sauce for the melon. You may make the Salsa or buy some of the "store bought fresh." The bacon is cooking while the pancakes are being mixed. We often use colorful paper plates if all seventeen family members are present. This sausage casserole has been featured for so many years that I often substitute a new and different "find" such as some of the others in this section. Use your imagination and swap these menu items around.

## Orange Butter

1/2 cup (1 stick) unsalted
   butter, softened
2 tablespoons
   confectioners' sugar
1 tablespoon grated
   orange zest
2 tablespoons orange juice
1/4 teaspoon vanilla
   extract
1/8 teaspoon nutmeg
Pinch of salt

Combine the butter,
confectioners' sugar, orange
zest, orange juice, vanilla,
nutmeg and salt in a food
processor and process
until smooth. Serve with
pancakes, biscuits or rolls.

*Yield: 3/4 cup*

# Sausage and Egg Casserole

*My favorite sister (my only one) lives in Atlanta and also serves this
often to her family. It's called "The Family Casserole."*

8 slices bread, crusts
   trimmed
1 pound mild or medium
   bulk pork sausage
1 teaspoon prepared mustard
1 cup (4 ounces) shredded
   sharp Cheddar cheese
1 cup milk
3/4 cup light cream
3 eggs, lightly beaten
1 teaspoon Worcestershire
   sauce
1/2 teaspoon salt
1/8 teaspoon pepper
1/4 tsp. nut meg

Arrange the bread in the bottom of a buttered
9×13-inch baking dish. Brown the sausage in
a skillet, stirring until crumbly; drain. Return
the sausage to the skillet. Stir in the prepared
mustard. Spread over the bread and sprinkle
with the cheese. You may freeze at this point.
Thaw completely before continuing. Combine
the milk, cream, eggs, Worcestershire sauce,
salt and pepper in a bowl and mix well. Pour
over the prepared layers. Refrigerate, covered,
overnight. Remove from the refrigerator 1 hour
before baking. Bake at 350 degrees for 30 to
35 minutes or until brown and bubbly. Serve
with salsa or fresh chopped tomatoes on top.
uncovered
*Yield: 10 servings*

# Salsa

4 tomatoes, seeded, chopped
2 jalapeño chiles, seeded,
   minced
1/2 cup minced onion
1/3 cup finely chopped green
   bell pepper
4 garlic cloves, minced
2 tablespoons olive oil
1 tablespoon fresh lemon or
   lime juice
1/4 cup minced fresh cilantro
1/2 teaspoon oregano
Salt and pepper to taste

Combine the tomatoes, jalapeño chiles,
onion, bell pepper, garlic, olive oil, lemon
juice, cilantro, oregano, salt and pepper in a
bowl and mix well. Chill, covered, until serving
time. Serve as an accompaniment to Sausage
and Egg Casserole (above) or as a dip with
tortilla chips.

*Yield: (about) 2 cups*

# Honey Nut Granola

2 1/2 cups rolled oats
1/2 cup sunflower seeds
1/2 cup whole almonds
1/3 cup honey
1 teaspoon vanilla extract
1/2 cup packed brown sugar
1/3 cup butter
1 teaspoon cinnamon
1/4 cup bran or wheat germ
1/3 cup each of 3 dried
   fruits such as raisins,
   sliced apricots,
   cherries, cranberries
   or banana chips

Combine the oats, sunflower seeds and almonds in a large bowl and mix well. Combine the honey, vanilla, brown sugar, butter and cinnamon in a saucepan. Cook over low heat until the brown sugar dissolves and the butter melts, stirring frequently. Stir in the bran. Pour over the oat mixture and stir until well coated. Spoon into a 9×13-inch baking pan. Bake at 350 degrees for 20 to 25 minutes or until lightly toasted, stirring occasionally. Remove the granola to a large bowl to cool completely, stirring frequently. Add the dried fruit and mix well.

*Yield: 5 to 6 cups*

# Melon with Raspberries and Cream

8 ounces tub-style cream
   cheese
1 cup vanilla yogurt
2 tablespoons honey
1 small cantaloupe, seeded,
   peeled, cut into thin
   wedges
1 small honeydew melon,
   seeded, peeled, cut into
   thin wedges
2 cups fresh raspberries

Combine the cream cheese, yogurt and honey in a food processor and process until smooth. Spoon into a bowl and refrigerate, covered, until serving time. Arrange the cantaloupe and honeydew wedges in fan shapes on individual dessert plates. Stir the cream cheese mixture and spoon over the melon wedges. Top each with about 1/4 cup of the raspberries. Refrigerate any leftover cream cheese mixture. May serve on a large serving platter, layering in the same order. May substitute blueberries for the raspberries.

*Yield: 8 to 10 servings*

## Metty's Pancakes

*This recipe may
be doubled or tripled.*

1 1/2 cups flour
1 tablespoon baking
   powder
1 tablespoon sugar
1/2 teaspoon salt
1 egg
1 3/4 cups milk
2 tablespoons canola oil

Combine the flour, baking powder, sugar and salt in a 2-quart bowl and mix well. Beat the egg in a small bowl. Blend in the milk. Add to the dry ingredients and mix well. Add the canola oil and mix well. Pour 1/4 cup of the batter at a time onto a hot, lightly greased griddle. Cook until brown on both sides, turning once. May add blueberries or sliced bananas to the top of the pancake before turning.

*Yield: (about)16 pancakes*

# An Island Breakfast

*Tropical Sangria • Guava Juice*
*Fresh Fruit with Honey Dressing*
*Island French Toast • Breakfast Frittata*
*Bacon and Cheddar Drop Biscuits • Ham*

Let's pretend that we are in the Islands. Maybe Hawaii, where I picked up this menu and then duplicated it on returning home. For decoration, place a beautiful orchid plant in the center of a basket, add some greenery and moss around the pot top. You could substitute a big bowl of strawberries instead of the assorted marinated cut fruit. Fruit may be prepared the day before and refrigerated. Even the Breakfast Frittata and the Bacon and Cheddar Drop Biscuits may be prepared the afternoon before. Refrigerate both, covered, before baking. The French toast ingredients need to be mixed up just before baking and serving. Remove the frittata and Cheddar biscuits an hour before baking. Bake the frittata and French toast plus biscuits at the last minute. Pour the mimosas. We were recently in Hawaii with our good friends the Swansons, the Jochims, the Rices, and the Vigelands at an orthopaedic meeting on the "Big Island." What delicious island food we had—especially the breakfasts. Many mornings we enjoyed the Island French Toast, sprinkled with macadamia nuts accompanied by coconut syrup. All of our breakfasts were outdoors on the terrace since the weather was so delightful. Another added treat was being able to see the humpback whales cavorting and blowing, just offshore in plain view from the beach or from our rooms in the hotel, the lovely Mauna Lani.

# Fresh Fruit with Honey Dressing

3 Granny Smith apples
3 Red Delicious apples
1 fresh pineapple
1 large cantaloupe
1 bunch seedless grapes
Orange juice
1 cup honey
1 cup lime juice
1/4 teaspoon ginger
Sliced fresh strawberries
  (optional)

Cut the apples, pineapple and cantaloupe into bite-size pieces. Combine with the grapes in a large bowl and toss to mix. Pour in enough orange juice to cover the fruit. Marinate, covered, for 1 hour or longer in the refrigerator. Drain the fruit, discarding the orange juice. Combine the honey, lime juice and ginger in a small bowl and mix well. Pour over the fruit and mix gently. Refrigerate, covered, until serving time. Top with the sliced strawberries just before serving.

*Yield: 6 to 8 servings*

# Island French Toast

1 (14-ounce) can sweetened
  coconut milk
1 French baguette
6 eggs
2 cups milk or half-and-half
2 tablespoons sugar
1 teaspoon coconut extract
1 teaspoon vanilla extract
1/2 cup flaked coconut
2 bananas, sliced
1/2 cup chopped macadamia
  nuts

Pour the sweetened coconut milk into a small saucepan. Warm over low heat, stirring occasionally. Cut the bread into 18 equal slices. Beat the eggs, milk, sugar, coconut extract and vanilla together in a large bowl. Dip the bread slices into the egg mixture and arrange on a well greased, insulated baking sheet. Pour any remaining egg mixture over the slices and let stand for 10 minutes. Sprinkle with 1/2 of the flaked coconut. Bake at 400 degrees for 7 minutes; turn. Top with the bananas and remaining flaked coconut. Bake for 8 to 12 minutes longer or until the toast and coconut are light brown but still slightly soft. Arrange 3 slices toast on each serving plate. Top with the warm coconut milk and macadamia nuts. Garnish with fresh raspberries and a dollop of sweetened whipped cream. You may substitute maple syrup for the sweetened coconut milk.

*Yield: 6 servings*

# Tropical Sangria

1 ripe mango,
  thinly sliced
1 lime, thinly sliced
1 lemon, thinly sliced
1/2 pineapple, cut into
  wedges, thinly sliced
1 star fruit (carambola),
  sliced
3 tablespoons sugar
1 bottle Champagne

Layer the mango, lime, lemon, pineapple and star fruit in a large punch bowl. Sprinkle with the sugar. Let stand for 30 minutes. Pour in the Champagne and stir gently just before serving.

*Yield: 4 to 8 servings*

# Breakfast Frittata

1 tablespoon butter
2 medium baking potatoes,
    peeled, thinly sliced
Salt to taste
1 cup (4 ounces) shredded
    Cheddar cheese
1/2 cup (2 ounces) shredded
    Swiss cheese
1 cup sour cream
2 tablespoons chopped
    chives
1 tablespoon butter
6 eggs, beaten
Pepper to taste
1 large tomato, peeled, sliced
2 tablespoons grated
    Parmesan cheese

Melt 1 tablespoon butter in a large skillet over medium-high heat. Add the potatoes and sauté until tender, stirring constantly. Sprinkle with salt. Remove the potatoes to a buttered 9-inch quiche pan. Sprinkle with 1/2 of the Cheddar cheese and 1/2 of the Swiss cheese. Spread with the sour cream and sprinkle with the chives. Melt 1 tablespoon butter in the skillet. Add the eggs and cook just until softly scrambled. Season with salt and pepper. Spread the eggs over the chives in the prepared dish. Top with the remaining Cheddar and Swiss cheeses. Arrange the tomato slices around the outer edge of the dish. Sprinkle the Parmesan cheese over the tomato. Bake at 400 degrees for 35 minutes or until puffed and light brown.

*Yield: 6 to 8 servings*

*Breakfast Frittata may be prepared one day ahead and refrigerated before adding the tomato and Parmesan cheese and baking. Your friends and family will love this. You might try leaving the tomato off before baking and sprinkling the finished dish with chopped fresh tomato just before serving.*

# Bacon and Cheddar Drop Biscuits

4 slices lean bacon
1/4 cup minced onion
Freshly ground pepper
    to taste
13/4 cups flour
2 teaspoons baking powder
1/2 teaspoon baking soda
1/2 teaspoon salt
2 tablespoons chilled
    shortening
3/4 cup shredded extra-sharp
    Cheddar cheese
2/3 cup milk

Cook the bacon in a skillet until crisp. Drain on paper towels, reserving 2 tablespoons of the bacon drippings in the skillet. Add the onion and cook over medium-low heat until tender, stirring frequently. Remove from the heat to cool. Crumble the bacon finely and place in a small bowl. Add the onion mixture and mix well. Season with pepper. Sift the flour, baking powder, baking soda and salt into a large bowl. Cut in the shortening until crumbly. Stir in the bacon mixture and cheese. Add the milk and stir just until a soft sticky dough forms. Drop the dough by rounded tablespoonfuls onto a greased baking sheet. Bake at 425 degrees for 15 to 17 minutes or until pale golden brown.

*Yield: (about) 16 biscuits*

# Home for the Holidays Brunch

*Warm Spiced Cider • Orange Blush*
*Praline Bacon • Italian Cheese and Vegetable Strata*
*Marinated Spiced Fruit*
*Raspberry and Lemon Muffins • Gingerbread Scones*

When everyone invades for the holidays we need to have things ready. What a brunch menu! Everything can be prepared ahead. Even the Praline Bacon can be partially prepared ahead. Early on the "day of" your brunch, place the bacon on a broiler pan which has been lightly sprayed and cook bacon until it begins to brown. Remove from oven, add sugar mixture to top and sprinkle with pecans. Set aside to finish cooking at the last minute. Stir up Orange Blush in a pitcher and refrigerate the day before. Also prepare Italian Cheese and Vegetable Strata, Marinated Spiced Fruit, muffins, and scones. The muffins and scones may be baked and reheated at time of serving. This strata makes a very good selection for a casual supper also. It is a great vegetarian dish. I love the flavor of the Asiago and provolone cheeses, both Italian cheeses. The Asiago cheese has a rich, nutty flavor. Your breakfast room or dining table probably has a Christmas greenery wreath with a globe, brass candlestick, and candle already, as a centerpiece. If not already decorated, buy the brightest apples you can find, core them and dip them into crystal clear floor wax. When they have dried, put a white candle in the cored area for candleholders. Place pine down the center of the table with candleholders among it. Another centerpiece could be a bowl lined with greenery and holding oranges studded with cloves in a pattern. To create a festive scent, combine cinnamon sticks, whole cloves, bay leaves, whole nutmeg, lemon and orange peels, and some water to cover in a saucepan. Place on low heat on the stovetop. Let it simmer. As the water evaporates, add more. Store in a quart jar in your refrigerator for later use.

- *Invite guests to your "soiree" early.*

- *Make your "to do" list. Decorate and bake items that can be frozen early.*

- *Stock up with nonperishables such as cocktail napkins, candles, film, toilet tissue, cleaning supplies, etc. so that all you need to buy at the last minute is fresh goods.*

- *Use the freezer. Bake cookies early; freeze. Crostini, pies, cakes, and rolls freeze easily.*

- *Create a decorating plan. My sweet friend, Jo Hosey, comes over and helps me decorate. She is so talented.*

# Warm Spiced Cider

8 cups apple cider
1/4 cup sugar
1 medium orange, thinly sliced
1 lemon, thinly sliced
1 lime, thinly sliced
2 (3-inch) cinnamon sticks
12 whole allspice
8 whole cloves

Combine the apple cider, sugar, orange, lemon, lime, cinnamon sticks, allspice and cloves in a 3-quart saucepan and mix well. Simmer over low heat for 24 minutes, stirring occasionally; do not boil. Strain the mixture, discarding the solids. Divide among 8 serving mugs. Garnish each with an orange slice and cinnamon stick.

*Yield: 8 servings*

# Orange Blush

4 cups orange juice
4 cups cranapple juice

Combine the orange juice and cranapple juice in a large pitcher and stir to mix. Pour over ice in glasses. Ginger ale may be added for a little extra zip.

*Yield: 8 servings*

# Praline Bacon

*This recipe is a winner, so I had to include it. Just try it, you will be surprised.*

1 pound thick-sliced bacon (12 slices)
3 tablespoons sugar
1 1/2 teaspoons chili powder
1/4 cup finely chopped pecans

Arrange the bacon in a single layer on a broiler rack in a broiler pan. Bake on the middle oven rack at 425 degrees for 10 minutes or just until the bacon begins to turn golden brown. Sprinkle with a mixture of the sugar and chili powder. Sprinkle with the pecans. Bake for 5 minutes longer or until brown and crisp. Drain praline side up on paper towels.

*Yield: 6 servings*

# Italian Cheese and Vegetable Strata

*Actually, if you're in a "twit" and must mix this up the morning of your brunch, it works almost as well. Just allow an hour for the egg-milk mixture to soak into the bread before baking. Be sure and shred your cheeses in the food processor, using the shredder disk.*

3 tablespoons olive oil
1 medium fennel bulb, trimmed, chopped
1 medium onion, thinly sliced
4 garlic cloves, sliced
1 (14-ounce) can diced tomatoes
1 tablespoon Dijon mustard
8 cups coarsely chopped fresh spinach
1/4 teaspoon salt
1/4 teaspoon pepper
1/4 teaspoon oregano
12 slices firm white bread, crusts removed
1/3 pound shredded asiago cheese (about 1 1/4 cups)
1/3 pound shredded provolone cheese (about 1 1/4 cups)
3 cups milk
5 eggs

Heat the olive oil in a large skillet over medium heat. Add the fennel and sauté for 1 minute. Add the onion and sauté for 8 to 10 minutes or until the onion and fennel are light brown. Add the garlic and cook for 1 minute longer. Stir in the tomatoes and Dijon mustard. Cook for 10 to 12 minutes or until the tomatoes soften, stirring frequently. Stir in the spinach, salt, pepper and oregano and cook for 1 minute longer. Remove from the heat. Cool for 10 minutes. Arrange 1/2 of the bread in the bottom of a 9×13-inch baking dish sprayed with nonstick cooking spray. Top with 1/2 of the vegetable mixture, 1/2 of the asiago cheese and 1/2 of the provolone cheese. Layer with the remaining bread, vegetable mixture and cheeses. Beat the milk and eggs together lightly in a large bowl. Pour over the prepared layers. Cover tightly with plastic wrap and refrigerate overnight. Bake, uncovered, at 350 degrees for 20 to 40 minutes or until the center appears set. Serve immediately.

*Yield: 12 servings*

## Tips for Holiday Entertaining

• *Allow others to bring items to help out with the menus. If family or friends offer to bring something, such as wine, a pumpkin pie, or casserole, let them.*

• *Clean your house early or bring in a housecleaning service. You will have more time to focus on baking and gift wrapping at the last minute.*

• *Have club soda on hand for quick rug cleanup.*

• *Work in a "workout." It helps with stress. Exercise produces endorphins, which boost your ability to withstand stress.*

• *Play holiday music to relax you.*

# Marinated Spiced Fruit

*Refreshing and flavorful. Vary the fruit with the season.*

1 small pineapple
1 small cantaloupe
3 large apples, peeled,
    cut into 1/3-inch chunks
3 large navel oranges,
    sectioned
Spiced Marinade (below)
1 pint strawberries sliced

Cut the pineapple into small wedges. Cut the cantaloupe into wedges or use a melon baller. Combine the pineapple, cantaloupe, apples and oranges in a large bowl. You should have approximately 2 cups of each fruit. Pour Spiced Marinade over the fruit. Refrigerate, covered, for several hours or overnight until serving time. Stir in the strawberries and garnish with mint leaves just before serving.

*Yield: 12 servings*

# Spiced Marinade

1/2 cup sugar
1 cup water
1/2 teaspoon lemon juice
2 cinnamon sticks
1/2 teaspoon whole cloves
1/2 teaspoon whole allspice
1/2 cup kirsch (optional)

Combine the sugar, water, lemon juice and cinnamon sticks in a small saucepan and mix well. Place the cloves and allspice in a piece of cheesecloth and secure with kitchen twine. Add to the sugar mixture. Bring to a boil over medium heat, stirring constantly. Lower the heat. Simmer, covered, for 5 minutes. Remove from the heat to cool. Remove the cinnamon sticks and spice bag. Stir in the kirsch.

# Gingerbread Scones

2 cups flour
3 tablespoons brown sugar
2 teaspoons baking powder
1/2 teaspoon baking soda
1/2 teaspoon salt
1 teaspoon ginger
1/2 teaspoon cinnamon
1/4 cup (1/2 stick) cold butter
1/3 cup molasses
1/4 cup milk
1 egg yolk
1 egg white
1/4 cup sugar

Combine the flour, brown sugar, baking powder, baking soda, salt, ginger, cinnamon and butter in a food processor. Cut in the butter by pulsing a few times until the mixture is crumbly. Remove to a medium bowl. Whisk the molasses, milk and egg yolk together in a small bowl. Stir into the flour mixture just until moistened. Knead gently 6 times on a floured surface. Roll 1/2 inch thick. Cut with a star-shaped cookie cutter. Arrange on a greased baking sheet. Beat the egg white in a small bowl until frothy. Brush over the scones. Sprinkle with the sugar. Bake at 400 degrees for 12 to 15 minutes or until golden brown. You may use parchment paper or a reusable Silpat pan liner instead of greasing the baking sheet.

*Yield: 20 scones*

## A Great Muffin

*The secret to good tender muffins is to not overmix. Also, gently fold in the berries. You can freeze the berries quickly and then stir them in with good results.*

# Raspberry and Lemon Muffins

2 cups flour
1 teaspoon baking powder
1 teaspoon baking soda
1/2 teaspoon salt
1 1/4 cups plain yogurt
2 eggs
1 teaspoon vanilla extract
1 tablespoon canola oil
2 dashes of cinnamon
2 teaspoons grated
    lemon zest
2 cups fresh or frozen
    raspberries

Sift the flour, baking powder, baking soda and salt into a large bowl. Combine the yogurt and eggs in a large bowl and mix well. Stir in the vanilla, canola oil, cinnamon and lemon zest. Add to the dry ingredients and stir just until moistened. Do not overmix. Fold in the raspberries gently. Spoon into greased or paper-lined muffin cups. Bake at 350 degrees for 15 to 20 minutes or until the muffins spring back when lightly touched. May use only the whites of the eggs if desired.

*Yield: 12 muffins or 24 miniature muffins*

# New Orleans Brunch

*Milk Punch • Orange Juice*
*Mimosas • Mock Turtle Soup*
*Eggs Sardou with Hollandaise*
*Orange Almond Scones with Mock Devonshire Cream*
*Creamy Swiss Grits • Bananas Foster*

This New Orleans Brunch menu is a great one to serve from the kitchen—exemplifying the new casual type of entertaining. The countdown is as follows—a couple of days ahead, buy groceries and plan centerpieces. Mardi Gras masks might accentuate your greenery or flowers. Be sure your eggs that you buy are nice and fresh for the Eggs Sardou. Poach eggs if you desire, one day ahead and place them in a bowl of cold water and refrigerate. Make your Orange Almond Scones a day ahead, cover with plastic wrap, and refrigerate. Of course, you can make them the "day of" and they will probably be a tiny bit more fluffy. Make your Mock Devonshire Cream and refrigerate. Prepare grits but do not bake, then refrigerate. These also may be prepared on the "day of." Place ice cream in bowls and put in freezer (if room). Mock Turtle Soup is actually better made the day before so that flavors can meld. A day ahead, set out plates, silverware, napkins, glassware, pitchers, and serving pieces. The "day of," a few hours ahead, fry the Canadian bacon, slice English muffins and butter lightly. Two hours ahead, remove scones from the refrigerator. Set eggs out and prepare to warm them at the last minute. Make Hollandaise and keep warm in a thermos bottle. Take grits out of refrigerator and set oven. Just before serving, bake grits, warm turtle soup, toast English muffins, warm eggs. Assemble Eggs Sardou and place on a large platter. Next, place everything on the buffet or table. If you are placing on a buffet, have soup in tureen with small bowls placed next to tureen. Next would come eggs, grits, asparagus, and Orange Almond Scones with Mock Devonshire Cream. Of course, a tray of water would be in order. Everyone can hold their plate or you can set tables to accommodate.

# Milk Punch

10 ounces bourbon, brandy
  or scotch
3 cups half-and-half or milk
3 tablespoons confectioners'
  sugar
2 teaspoons vanilla extract
Nutmeg to taste

Combine the bourbon, half-and-half, confectioners' sugar and vanilla in a container with a tight fitting lid. Shake until blended. Pour into 8-ounce highball glasses. Sprinkle with nutmeg. You may use artificial sweetener and skim milk for a slim version.

*Yield: 8 servings*

# Mimosas

2 (8-ounce) cans frozen
  orange juice concentrate,
  thawed
1 (10-ounce) jar maraschino
  cherries with stems,
  drained
2 (750-milliliter) bottles dry
  Champagne, chilled

Prepare the orange juice concentrate using the can directions. Pour 1/2 of the orange juice into two 12-cube ice cube trays. Chill the remaining orange juice. Place 1 cherry in each cube. Freeze for 8 hours. Combine the Champagne and chilled orange juice in a pitcher and stir to mix. Pour over the orange ice cubes in glasses.

*Yield: 3 quarts*

# I Love New Orleans

Our entire family, along with our dear friends and former neighbors, the Coles and also the Gesslings, invaded the city for the Sugar Bowl, Tennessee vs. Auburn. Bill and I are Tennessee alumni and three of our children are Auburn graduates. What a great time and, of course, we had breakfast at Brennan's and I had Eggs Sardou. We all stayed at a lovely old inn in the French Quarter.

*This New Orleans menu was created for a fall cooking class which Bay Naylor and I taught together. Bay is a Louisiana native and a Cajun cook and we have been friends for many years—from medical school days. Bay is one of those cooks that adds "a little of this and a little of that" and the end result is super. Bay gives you a quicker way to prepare "roux" for turtle soup, gumbos, or other recipes using browned flour.*

*Bill and I have hosted groups on New Year's Day and other times, using this menu. We have substituted Conecuh sausage that Barney Lovelace furnishes us from South Alabama for the Canadian bacon. Yummy!*

# Mock Turtle Soup

*Bay and I priced turtle meat, which we planned to have shipped to us, and were astounded to learn that eight pounds of turtle meat would have cost over one-hundred dollars. So much for that idea. So here you have the "mock" version using beef.*

1 cup flour
1 (3-pound) beef sirloin tip roast, minced
2 garlic cloves, minced
1 onion, finely chopped
6 cups water
1 red bell pepper, finely chopped
1 green bell pepper, finely chopped
1 (26-ounce) jar Italian garlic and herb spaghetti sauce
1 cup ketchup
1/2 cup Worcestershire sauce
2 tablespoons Dale's steak sauce
3 quarts water
1 teaspoon minced fresh sage
1 tablespoon minced fresh parsley
1 teaspoon dillweed
2 teaspoons Tony Chachere's Creole seasoning
1/2 teaspoon minced garlic
3 hard-cooked eggs, chopped

Microwave the flour in a microwave-safe dish on High for 6 minutes, stopping at 2-minute intervals to stir. Microwave on High for 3 minutes longer, stopping at 30-second intervals to stir; set aside. Brown the beef with 2 minced garlic cloves and the onion in a skillet until the beef is brown and the onion is translucent, stirring constantly; set aside. Pour 6 cups water into a 4-quart saucepan. Add the bell peppers, spaghetti sauce, ketchup, Worcestershire sauce and steak sauce and mix well. Bring to a boil and reduce the heat. Simmer for 20 minutes, stirring occasionally. Place the browned flour in a large heavy stockpot. Add 3 quarts water and stir with a whisk. Add the beef mixture and vegetable sauce and mix well. Add the sage, parsley, dillweed, Creole seasoning, 1/2 teaspoon minced garlic and the eggs and mix well. Simmer for 1 hour or longer, stirring frequently. Ladle into soup bowls to serve.

*Yield: 16 servings*

## Tara

*I have the most adorable daughter-in-law, Tara Ball Sims, who is a joy and hails from Baton Rouge, Louisiana. She is a great Cajun cook also and recently had a wonderful seafood gumbo for my birthday lunch. The secret is the roux.*

# Eggs Sardou

*Eggs may also be poached in custard cups in a skillet. Brush the inside of the custard cups with vegetable oil. Break 1 egg into each cup and arrange the cups in a large skillet. Pour in enough water to come halfway up the sides of the cups. Simmer gently, covered, for about 6 minutes. Run a knife around the edge of the custard cups to loosen the eggs for easy release. It is very easy to use the new electric egg poachers. I have two poachers that poach four eggs at a time. I feel that the poached eggs are much better if done at the time of serving instead of storing in cold water.*

16 slices Canadian bacon
  or ham
Butter
16 eggs
8 English muffins, split,
  lightly toasted
Artichoke bottoms (optional)
2 (10-ounce) packages frozen
  creamed spinach,
  prepared
2 recipes Hollandaise
  (at right)
Paprika, salt, and pepper
  to taste

Sauté the Canadian bacon in a small amount of butter in a skillet until light brown. Drain on paper towels. Bring 3 to 4 inches of lightly salted water to a boil in a large saucepan. Reduce the temperature to a slow simmer. Break the eggs 1 at a time into a cup and gently slide each egg into the water. Poach 2 or 3 eggs at a time for 3 to 5 minutes or until done to taste. Remove with a slotted spoon and drain on paper towels. Butter the muffin halves and arrange on a serving plate. Top with the Canadian bacon, artichoke bottoms, poached eggs and creamed spinach. Pour Hollandaise over the top. Sprinkle with paprika, salt and pepper. Garnish with sprigs of parsley.

*Yield: 8 servings*

## Hollandaise

1 cup (2 sticks) butter
6 egg yolks
3/4 teaspoon salt
Juice of 1 1/2 lemons

Microwave the butter in a microwave-safe bowl until melted and bubbling. Combine the egg yolks, salt and lemon juice in a food processor and process until smooth. Add the bubbling hot butter, processing continuously until thickened. Keep warm in a thermos. So easy!

*Yield: About 2 cups*

## Mock Devonshire Cream

2 cups sour cream
1/2 cup sugar
1 tablespoon lemon juice

Combine the sour cream, sugar and lemon juice in a bowl and mix well. Refrigerate, covered, until ready to use.

*Yield: 2 1/2 cups*

# Orange Almond Scones

*These are absolutely delicious and just as good the following day. Reheat in the microwave.*

1 to 2 oranges
1/4 cup buttermilk, plain yogurt or milk
1 egg
1/4 teaspoon almond extract
3 cups flour
1/2 cup sugar
4 teaspoons baking powder
1/2 teaspoon baking soda
1/4 teaspoon salt
1/2 cup (1 stick) cold unsalted butter, cut into 8 pieces
1/2 cup finely chopped blanched almonds

Grate enough zest from the oranges to measure 1 tablespoon; set aside. Squeeze enough juice from the oranges to measure 1/2 cup. Pour the orange juice into a 2-cup glass measure. Add the buttermilk, egg and almond extract and beat with a fork until smooth. Combine the flour, sugar, baking powder, baking soda and salt in a food processor and process until mixed. Cut in the butter by pulsing until the mixture is crumbly. Remove to a bowl. Add the almonds and orange zest and toss to distribute evenly. Add the egg mixture and stir with a fork until a soft dough forms. Knead 5 or 6 times on a lightly floured surface or just until well mixed. Shape the dough into a ball. Roll 1/2 inch thick. Cut with a heart-shaped cookie cutter. Arrange the scones on a greased baking sheet. Bake at 375 degrees for 20 minutes or until medium-brown. Cool on a wire rack. Serve with Devonshire Cream (at left).

*Yield: 20 scones*

# Creamy Swiss Grits

4 cups milk
1 cup grits
1/2 cup chopped scallions
1/2 cup (1 stick) butter,
  softened
1 egg, beaten
1 teaspoon salt
1/2 teaspoon white pepper
1/3 cup butter, softened
4 ounces Swiss or Gruyère
  cheese, shredded
1/2 cup freshly grated
  Parmesan cheese

Bring the milk to a boil over medium heat in a saucepan, stirring frequently. Add the grits, scallions and 1/2 cup butter and mix well. Cook for 5 minutes or until the mixture is the consistency of oatmeal, stirring constantly. Remove from the heat. Add a small amount of the hot milk mixture to the egg in a cup. Add the egg mixture to the hot milk mixture in the saucepan. Stir in the salt and white pepper. Add 1/3 cup butter and the Swiss cheese and mix well. Spoon into a greased 2-quart baking dish. Sprinkle with the Parmesan cheese. Bake at 350 degrees for 1 hour.

*Yield: 10 servings*

# Bananas Foster

1/2 gallon French vanilla ice
  cream
1/3 cup butter
1 cup packed brown sugar
1 teaspoon cinnamon
2 large bananas
1/3 cup banana liqueur
1/2 cup kirsch

Scoop the ice cream into individual dessert bowls and freeze. Melt the butter slowly in a heavy skillet or flambé pan. Add the brown sugar and cinnamon and mix well. Cook slowly over low heat until the mixture bubbles. Cut the bananas into thirds. Cut each third into halves lengthwise. Arrange the bananas, cut side down, in the sauce. Cook over low heat just until the bananas are tender, spooning the hot sauce over the bananas frequently. Add the banana liqueur and heat until bubbly. Pour the kirsch over the sauce and ignite carefully. Spoon over the ice cream and serve immediately.

*Yield: 4 to 6 servings*

*Once when we were having our neighbors, the Bounds, over for dinner, I was flambéeing at the table and when I poured the kirsch over the bananas, I got some on my hand and ignited my hand—no harm done—the "show went on."*

# An Elegant Brunch

*Champagne • Sparkling Grape Juice*
*Virgin Marys • Poached Spiced Pears*
*Oeufs and Champignons*
*Asparagus with Orange and Cashews*
*Cream Cheese Brunch Cake*

The preparation of this elegant brunch may be done ahead of your date with a minimum of trouble. Your buffet table and tables for seating could be decorated with flowers or greenery in a series of silver mint julep cups with a lovely silk ribbon tied at the base of each silver cup. These would be most attractive down the center of the table, using at least five cups. The egg and mushroom casserole can be prepared the day before and refrigerated as can the pears and the brunch cake. The asparagus may be blanched the day before, cooled, patted dry, and refrigerated between paper towels. Just before you serve, remove asparagus from refrigerator and follow the recipe directions for orange sauce. A couple of hours before you serve, remove the egg casserole from the refrigerator and set your oven. Bake the casserole. Warm the brunch cake, slice and put on your platter with a pretty doily or lovely napkin. Place pears in a crystal or attractive serving dish along with arranging the asparagus on the buffet. A day or two ahead assemble all of your glassware, flutes for Champagne, glasses for water, flatware, serving pieces, and napkins. If you plan to serve buffet style, my favorite, especially for a large group, place your water glasses on a silver tray and offer Champagne from a tray as guests arrive. Use small bright cocktail napkins. Place your fruit first, then main dish, asparagus next and your brunch cake last. Place appropriate serving pieces.

# Virgin Marys

*A classic breakfast or brunch drink that doesn't require the addition of alcohol to be delicious. Bloody Marys without alcohol are called Virgin Marys. Add a celery stalk with leaves to each glass.*

32 ounces tomato juice
Juice of 1 1/2 lemons
3/4 teaspoon freshly ground
   pepper
1/2 teaspoon salt
10 drops of Tabasco sauce
2 teaspoons Worcestershire
   sauce
1 tablespoon grated fresh
   horseradish

Combine the tomato juice, lemon juice, pepper, salt, Tabasco sauce, Worcestershire sauce and horseradish in a large pitcher or jar and stir or shake until blended. Pour into glasses.

*Yield: 10 servings*

# Poached Spiced Pears

10 firm ripe pears
4 cups water
2 teaspoons lemon juice
2/3 cup sugar
6 cinnamon sticks
Dash of freshly ground
   nutmeg
1/4 teaspoon salt

Peel and cut the pears into quarters, discarding the stems and cores. Place in a large saucepan. Add the water, lemon juice, sugar, cinnamon sticks, nutmeg and salt and stir to mix. Bring to a boil; reduce the heat. Simmer for 15 minutes or just until the pears are tender, stirring occasionally. Remove from the heat to cool. Drain the pears, discarding the liquid and cinnamon sticks. Refrigerate, covered, until ready to serve. Serve cold or reheated in the microwave.

*Yield: 10 to 12 servings*

*This menu is guaranteed to bring rave reviews. A coffee table would be in order with flavored whipped cream to adorn the java. Another idea would be to let an espresso-cappucino machine be the centerpiece of your coffee table. Place demitasse cups near with a shaker of cinnamon or nutmeg.*

# Oeufs and Champignons

12 hard-cooked eggs, peeled
1 pint fresh mushrooms, minced
1/4 cup (1/2 stick) butter
Salt, white pepper and red pepper to taste
Worcestershire sauce to taste
Tabasco sauce to taste
8 ounces sliced bacon, crisp-cooked, crumbled
12 ounces sharp Cheddar cheese, shredded
1/2 cup (1 stick) butter
1/2 cup flour
3 cups milk
1/4 cup sherry
2 tablespoons minced fresh parsley

Slice the eggs in half lengthwise. Remove and mash the yolks in a bowl until smooth. Sauté the mushrooms in 1/4 cup butter in a skillet until tender. Add 1/2 of the mushroom mixture to the egg yolks. Season generously with salt, white pepper, red pepper, Worcestershire sauce and Tabasco sauce, mixing until well combined. Spoon the mixture into the egg whites and press 2 halves at a time together to form whole eggs. Arrange in a lightly greased 2-quart round baking dish. Top with the remaining mushroom mixture, 1/2 of the bacon and 1/2 of the cheese. Melt 1/2 cup butter in a saucepan over medium heat. Add the flour and cook until bubbly, stirring constantly. Add the milk gradually, stirring until thickened. Season generously with salt, white pepper, red pepper, Worcestershire sauce and Tabasco sauce. Add the sherry and mix well. Pour over the prepared layers. Top with the remaining bacon and cheese. May be refrigerated, covered, at this point. Bring to room temperature. Bake at 350 degrees for 25 to 30 minutes or until bubbly. Sprinkle with the parsley. Garnish with paprika.

*Yield: 12 servings*

*My good friend Toby Sewell shared this recipe with me years ago. It has been served at many "Day of the Wedding" brunches and is so good. A lot of those "Day of the Wedding" brunches have been held at Jack and Toby's home, the lovely historic Belle Mina Mansion, Governor Bibbs' home built in 1826.*

# Asparagus with Orange and Cashews

2 pounds asparagus,
  trimmed
1/4 cup (1/2 stick) butter
2 tablespoons grated orange
  zest
6 ounces cashews

Blanch the asparagus in boiling water to cover in a stockpot for 7 minutes or just until tender. Drain and immediately refresh under cold running water. Drain and pat dry with paper towels. Melt the butter in a large skillet over medium heat. Add the orange zest and cashews and mix well. Add the asparagus and toss to coat until heated through. Serve warm or at room temperature.

*Yield: 6 to 8 servings*

# Cream Cheese Brunch Cake

1/2 cup (1 stick) butter,
  softened
2/3 cup sugar
1 egg
13/4 cups flour
1/2 teaspoon baking soda
1/4 teaspoon salt
11/2 cups buttermilk
16 ounces cream cheese,
  softened
Grated zest of 2 lemons
3/4 cup sugar
1 tablespoon butter
1 tablespoon flour
2 tablespoons lemon juice
1 egg

Beat 1/2 cup butter and 2/3 cup sugar in a bowl until light and fluffy. Add 1 egg and beat well. Sift 13/4 cups flour, the baking soda and salt together. Add to the creamed mixture alternately with the buttermilk, mixing well after each addition. Scrape the bowl. Pour the batter into a greased 9-inch cake pan. Beat the cream cheese in a mixing bowl until fluffy. Add the lemon zest, 3/4 cup sugar, 1 tablespoon butter, 1 tablespoon flour, the lemon juice and 1 egg and mix well. Pour carefully over the top of the cake batter. Bake at 350 degrees for 45 minutes or until the cake tests done. Cool. Cut into squares to serve.

*Yield: 6 to 8 servings*

*If you haven't used or purchased a new zester, called a "plainer," you must. They have a sharp blade surface and a handle and they give you zest in an instant.*

# A Casual Brunch for Friends

*Cranapple Juice • Winter Fruit Compote*
*Baked Eggs with Mushrooms and Caramelized Onions*
*Maple Pecan Bacon*
*Easy Potatoes and Colby Cheese*
*Popovers with Oven Apple Butter*

Invite your friends over for a delicious brunch, easy but very tasty. Put a pitcher of cranapple juice on a tray with juice glasses. They day before your brunch, make your Baked Eggs with Mushrooms and Caramelized Onions. Caramelized onions are really "big" right now. Caramelizing the onions brings a wonderful flavor to the dish. Refrigerate overnight. The potatoes could be mixed up and refrigerated before baking a day ahead, as can the Winter Fruit Compote. The apple butter could be cooked days ahead, cooled, and refrigerated (or buy some). Mix your popover batter up and let it stand an hour before baking popovers. The Maple Pecan Bacon should be cooked just before serving. Remove your Winter Fruit Compote from the refrigerator and heat just before serving. Use small crystal vases on the table with a single blossom in each. Use the same type of flower.

# Baked Eggs with Mushrooms and Caramelized Onions

1 pound mushrooms, sliced
6 tablespoons unsalted
   butter
1/2 teaspoon salt
1/2 teaspoon freshly ground
   black pepper
1 teaspoon lemon juice
10 tablespoons unsalted
   butter
3 tablespoons olive oil
4 medium onions, sliced
1 cup flour
1 quart milk
3/4 teaspoon salt
1/8 teaspoon each nutmeg,
   thyme and cayenne
   pepper
2/3 cup heavy cream or milk
16 hard-cooked eggs, peeled,
   sliced
1 1/2 cups (6 ounces)
   shredded Gruyère or
   Swiss cheese

Sauté the mushrooms in 6 tablespoons butter in a large skillet until tender. Add 1/2 teaspoon salt, the black pepper and lemon juice and mix well. Melt 10 tablespoons butter with the olive oil in a large saucepan over low heat. Add the onions and cook, covered, for 5 minutes. Increase the heat and cook, uncovered, until the onions are golden brown, stirring frequently. Whisk in the flour gradually. Add the milk and bring the mixture to a boil. Cook until thickened, whisking constantly. Add 3/4 teaspoon salt, the nutmeg, thyme and cayenne pepper. Add the cream, whisking to thin the sauce. Pour some of the cream sauce into a baking dish sprayed with nonstick cooking spray. Layer with the egg slices, remaining cream sauce and mushroom mixture. Sprinkle evenly with the cheese. Bake at 375 degrees for 15 to 20 minutes or until hot and bubbly.

*Yield: 8 to 10 servings*

## Popovers

6 eggs
2 cups milk
2 cups flour
6 tablespoons butter,
 melted
1/2 teaspoon salt

Combine the eggs, milk,
flour, butter and salt in a
large bowl and stir just
until blended. The batter
should be a little lumpy.
Fill buttered glass custard
cups 1/2 full. Arrange on
a baking sheet. Bake at
350 to 375 degrees for
45 minutes. Do not
open the oven until the
baking is complete. Serve
immediately with Orange
Butter (page 12), honey
or jam.

*Yield: 6 servings*

## Maple Pecan Bacon

1/4 cup maple syrup
8 slices thick-cut bacon
1 cup finely chopped pecans

Pour the syrup into a shallow bowl. Dip each
bacon slice into the syrup, allowing the excess
to drip back into the bowl. Arrange on a lightly
greased rack in a 10×15-inch baking pan or
on a broiler pan. Sprinkle with the pecans
and press to adhere. Bake at 400 degrees for
25 minutes or until brown, watching carefully
to prevent burning.

*Yield: 4 servings*

## Easy Potatoes and Colby Cheese

1 (26-ounce) package frozen
 country-style hash brown
 potatoes
2 cups (8 ounces) shredded
 Colby cheese
1/4 cup minced onion
1 cup milk
1/2 cup beef stock or canned
 beef broth
2 tablespoons butter, melted
Dash of garlic powder
1 teaspoon salt
1/4 teaspoon pepper

Combine the hash brown potatoes, cheese and
onion in a large bowl and mix well. Combine
the milk, beef stock, butter, garlic powder, salt
and pepper in a medium bowl and mix until
blended. Pour over the hash brown potato
mixture and mix well. Spoon into a 9×9-inch
glass baking dish. Microwave until the potatoes
are hot and the cheese is melted. Remove from
the microwave. Bake at 425 degrees until the
surface of the potatoes is brown.

*Yield: 6 to 8 servings*

# Winter Fruit Compote

2 cups white grape juice
1 cup water
3/4 cup sugar
2 (3-inch) cinnamon sticks
1 star anise
4 whole cloves
3 firm medium pears,
    peeled, cut into quarters
1 cup dried apricots,
    cut into halves
1 cup prunes
1/2 cup dried cranberries
1 large navel orange,
    sectioned

Combine the grape juice, water, sugar, cinnamon sticks, star anise and cloves in a 3-quart saucepan and mix well. Bring to a boil over medium heat. Reduce the heat to low. Add the pears, apricots, prunes and cranberries and stir gently. Simmer, covered, for 15 to 20 minutes or until the fruit has softened. Remove from the heat. Let stand for 15 minutes to cool. Remove and discard the cinnamon sticks, star anise and cloves. Pour the fruit mixture into a serving bowl. Add the orange sections and toss to mix just before serving or refrigerate until serving time and add the orange sections at the last minute.

*Yield: 12 servings*

# Oven Apple Butter

8 Granny Smith apples,
    peeled, chopped
1 cup apple juice
1 cup sugar
1 teaspoon cinnamon
1/2 teaspoon ground cloves
1/2 teaspoon salt

Combine the apples and apple juice in a Dutch oven. Cook over medium heat for 30 minutes or until the apples are tender, stirring occasionally. Stir until the apples are mashed. Stir in the sugar, cinnamon, cloves and salt. Pour into a lightly greased 7×11-inch baking dish. Bake at 275 degrees for 4 1/2 hours or until of spreading consistency, stirring every hour. Chill, covered, until ready to use.

*Yield: 3 cups*

*Store any leftover compote in an airtight container in the refrigerator for up to one week. Serve the compote as a side dish at room temperature or warm gently and serve with vanilla ice cream or pound cake for a delicious dessert.*

# A Southern Brunch

*Banana Berry Ambrosia*
*Spinach Sausage Brunch Bake*
*Herby Green Onion Boursin Spread*
*Easy Grits • Bonnie's Biscuits*
*Blueberry Crunch Coffee Ring*

This Southern Brunch, with grits, of course, and biscuits, has a slight Italian twist with Italian sausage in the casserole. The casserole may be assembled and refrigerated the day before your brunch as can the Banana Berry Ambrosia. The Blueberry Crunch Coffee Ring may be made a couple of days ahead. Plan to make the biscuits and Easy Grits in the last hour. Any southern gathering could certainly have magnolia leaves and blossoms (if available) just laid in the center of the table. Jackson Vine also adds to any southern occasion, says my daughter, Sheri. Just place vines in the center of the table and nestle a collection of animals among the greenery. Cotton blossoms and bolls certainly would add a southern touch as a centerpiece. By the way, the biscuits can be made early in the day and refrigerated before baking. Remove from the refrigerator an hour or so before baking. Be sure you have some Orange Butter (page 12) on hand or maybe just old-fashioned sorghum syrup is your weakness. My husband, Bill, loves it.

# Banana Berry Ambrosia

1 pint fresh raspberries
1 pint fresh blueberries
4 medium bananas, sliced
1/2 to 1 1/2 cups fresh
    orange juice
1/3 cup flaked coconut,
    toasted

Rinse the raspberries and blueberries. Drain well on paper towels. Arrange the banana slices in the bottom of a large glass serving bowl. Layer with the raspberries and blueberries. Pour the orange juice over the fruit. Refrigerate, covered, until thoroughly chilled. Top with the coconut just before serving.

*Yield: 8 (3/4-cup) servings*

# Spinach Sausage Brunch Bake

1 pound bulk sweet Italian
    sausage
1 cup chopped onion
1 (10-ounce) package frozen
    chopped spinach, thawed
1 red bell pepper, chopped
1 cup (4 ounces) shredded
    mozzarella cheese
1 cup (4 ounces) shredded
    Cheddar cheese
1 cup flour
1/2 cup freshly grated
    Parmesan cheese
1/2 teaspoon salt
8 eggs
2 cups milk

Brown the sausage with the onion in a skillet, stirring until the sausage is crumbly and the onion is tender; drain. Drain the spinach, squeezing out as much moisture as possible. Place the sausage mixture in a greased 9×13-inch baking dish. Sprinkle with 1/2 of the bell pepper. Top with the spinach. Layer with the mozzarella cheese, Cheddar cheese and remaining bell pepper. Combine the flour, Parmesan cheese and salt in a bowl and mix well. Beat the eggs and milk together in a bowl until smooth. Add to the flour mixture and mix well. Pour over the prepared layers. Bake at 425 degrees for 30 to 40 minutes or until a knife inserted in the center comes out clean. Let stand for 5 minutes. Cut into squares.

*Yield: 8 to 10 servings*

# Herby Green Onion Boursin Spread

6 ounces cream cheese, softened

1/4 cup mixed freshly chopped herbs such as parsley, dill weed, chives, basil or thyme

1 to 2 scallions, finely chopped

Salt and freshly ground pepper to taste

Beat the cream cheese in a small mixing bowl until smooth and fluffy. Add the herbs and scallions and mix well. Season with salt and pepper.

*Yield: About 1 cup*

*Never, never overknead biscuits. Kneading biscuits makes them tough. Another secret to light tender biscuits made in the South is White Lily Flour. This brand is made exclusively from soft wheat. My mother, Lois Brandon, was a wonderful cook and always used White Lily Flour. We had a great cook and friend at our house in Georgia through the years, Effie Jones, and she always added extra Crisco and made a really "short" biscuit. She never measured ingredients and those biscuits melted in your mouth. Of course, she used White Lily.*

# Bonnie's Biscuits

*Without a doubt, Bonnie Bailey's biscuits are the best southern biscuits. Bonnie is my friend from Birmingham, who owned Highland Gourmet, and who inspired me to open Johnston Street Cafe. She has a cookbook, Baking Secrets, which has been a great success.*

3 cups self-rising flour

2 tablespoons sugar

1/2 teaspoon salt

1/4 teaspoon baking powder

6 tablespoons shortening

2 cups heavy cream

1/2 cup buttermilk

Melted unsalted butter

Mix the self-rising flour, sugar, salt and baking powder in a large bowl. Cut in the shortening using a pastry blender. Add the cream and buttermilk and mix quickly with your hands or a fork. Shape the dough into balls using floured hands and working quickly. Arrange in 2 greased and lightly floured 9-inch baking pans with the dough balls touching. Bake at 425 degrees for 10 to 15 minutes or until golden brown. Brush the tops of the biscuits with melted butter.

*Yield: variable*

# Easy Grits

*Grits are to the South a cultural statement on a plate. Add hot red pepper sauce or black pepper for a blast of spiciness.*

6 cups milk
1 teaspoon salt
1¹/2 cups quick-cooking grits
1¹/2 cups (6 ounces)
    shredded Cheddar cheese
¹/2 cup (1 stick) butter

Bring the milk and salt to a boil in a large saucepan. Add the grits gradually, stirring constantly. Cook for 4 to 5 minutes or until done to taste, stirring frequently. Remove from the heat. Add the cheese and butter. Cook over low heat until the cheese and butter are melted, stirring constantly. Spoon into a serving bowl and sprinkle with additional cheese.

*Yield: 6 to 8 servings*

# Blueberry Crunch Coffee Ring

¹/2 cup finely chopped
    walnuts
¹/2 cup packed brown sugar
2 tablespoons flour
2 teaspoons cinnamon
2 tablespoons butter, melted
1¹/2 cups flour
³/4 cup sugar
1 tablespoon baking powder
¹/2 teaspoon salt
¹/4 teaspoon nutmeg
¹/3 cup butter
1 cup blueberries
1 egg
¹/2 cup milk or buttermilk
1 teaspoon vanilla extract

Mix the walnuts, brown sugar, 2 tablespoons flour, the cinnamon and 2 tablespoons melted butter in a bowl. Pat ¹/2 of the walnut streusel into the bottom of a greased and floured 9-inch tube pan. Combine 1¹/2 cups flour, the sugar, baking powder, salt and nutmeg in a large bowl and mix well. Cut in ¹/3 cup butter using a pastry blender until the mixture resembles coarse crumbs. Stir in the blueberries gently. Blend the egg, milk and vanilla together in a small bowl. Add to the blueberry mixture and stir just until combined. Spread ¹/2 of the mixture over the walnut streusel layer in the prepared pan. Layer with the remaining walnut streusel and blueberry mixture. Bake at 350 degrees for 45 to 60 minutes or until the cake tests done. Cool in the pan on a wire rack for 20 minutes. Invert onto a serving plate and dust with confectioners' sugar.

*Yield: 16 servings*

*According to the Encyclopedia of Southern Culture, when English settlers came ashore at Jamestown in 1607, they were greeted by Indians bearing grits or something similar. We have become quite used to cooking quick grits or instant grits, but actually, I prefer stone ground grits. They are so much more flavorful. Glenn Roberts at Anson Mills in Columbia, South Carolina, is organically growing heirloom varieties of corn and sending it around the world via Federal Express. Grits (stone-ground) are also sold at Calloway Gardens and through Williams-Sonoma.*

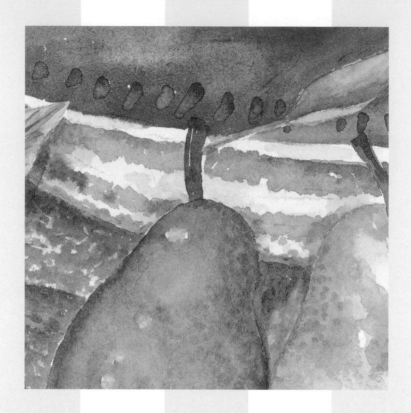

# *Luncheons*

# Menus

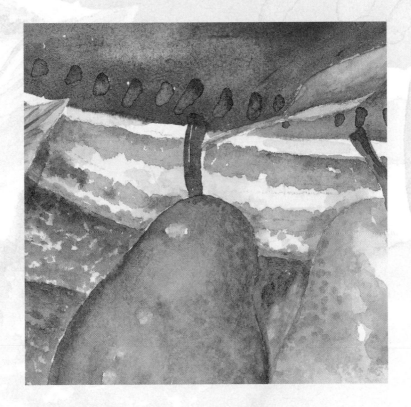

A Mother's Day Luncheon

A Book Club Luncheon

Remembering Johnston Street Cafe Luncheon

Bridesmaids' Luncheon

One of the most memorable luncheons that I have ever attended was the one that Martha Stewart gave for her mom at Turkey Hill Farm. I was attending a seminar in Westport, Connecticut, on "Entertaining" just after I opened Johnston Street Cafe. It was on the occasion of Martha's mother's birthday. Martha had each room set with a different china and very simple one-flower arrangements in crystal vases for the centerpieces at each table. Of course, just being there at Turkey Hill Farm was such a thrill and the food delicious although I've lost my notes on what exactly we did eat. There were 22 of us, all in the food business or at least aspiring to be. By the way, Martha is a perfectionist but is a very talented person and has given us all so much wonderful advice on the presentation of food and also on gardening and organizing.

If you are planning a luncheon, which I'm sure all of you will at some time or other, my rule of thumb is that if you have twelve or more persons, it is best to serve buffet style. Otherwise serve the plates from the kitchen.

Historically, a buffet meal was always laid out on a sideboard (the French word for this piece of furniture is still buffet). Guests help themselves from the food offered and carry it to the table or sit down with plates on their laps. If you plan a buffet for any of the meals, for many guests, a spectacular central display of food in a large room creates a gathering place and a talking point which helps put people at ease as they are standing in line.

In my years of entertaining at home and the many years at Johnston Street, I have staged multi multi luncheons. Some have been quite elegant, such as bridemaids' luncheons or wedding reception luncheons, and others have been as informal as picnic basket luncheons. At Johnston Street Cafe, our most favorite lunch plate was the chicken salad plate (the chicken salad made only with the tenders of the chicken, fruit salad with poppy seed dressing, a banana bread sandwich filled with orange cream cheese, and our famous homemade pickle). When I first opened Johnston Street, somewhat of a city concept, with a tearoom lunch area, complete deli for takeout, baskets, wine, and retail items, I was determined to serve very gourmet food. I was quick to realize that actually the most popular foods are "comfort foods"—so we came up with "meat loaf day" on Wednesday. The public loved it and we were always packed. My daughter, Sheri, was very pregnant and was going to be induced on a day of her choice. She called me and said, "When should we do this?" and I said, "If at all possible don't plan to have the baby on 'meat loaf day.'" Of course, I was being facetious but that's what popped into my mind.

In this section, I have provided both elegant menus and much less formal plans for your luncheons.

# A Mother's Day Luncheon

*Mint Tea • Tangerine Mimosas*
*Bacon Cheese Fingers*
*Dilled Squash Soup*
*Baby Bleu Salad • French Lasagna*
*Cinnamon Chocolate Brownies with Chocolate Ganache*

Definitely a "Do Ahead" menu. I would not freeze the French Lasagna since the béchamel sauce does not freeze well, but prepare the lasagna the day before and refrigerate uncooked. Bacon Cheese Fingers could be done ahead and frozen. The soup is much better if prepared the day before. All those flavors meld. The salad greens may be washed and stored in a sealable plastic bag, the pecans baked, cooled, and stored in an airtight container. Make the Balsamic Vinaigrette and refrigerate as much as four days ahead. Make your brownies if you like and freeze. They freeze beautifully. Don't forget to plan your presentation on the buffet. If you have a small group or family, you may prefer to serve the plates or serve family style at the table. Use wonderful paper plates in bright colors, pottery, or china. Set your table and use a bowl or tray filled with fresh vegetables as a simple centerpiece, or a simple bouquet of tulips in a low crystal bowl. Invite your mother for a special, easy-to-prepare luncheon or invite several mothers and daughters and celebrate spring or prepare this menu for your family on Mother's Day since it is a "snap"—that is if you're not lucky enough to be "taken out" on your day to celebrate.

## Tangerine Mimosas

3 to 4 tangerines
3 cups fresh tangerine
  juice, chilled
1 (750-milliliter) bottle
  Champagne or
  sparkling wine, chilled

Peel the tangerines using
a vegetable peeler or thin
sharp knife, creating
12 spirals, each about
6 inches long. Place each
spiral in a chilled cham-
pagne flute. Fill each
halfway with the tangerine
juice (about 2 ounces
each). Fill each flute
almost to the top with
the Champagne (about
2 ounces each). Stir gently
with an up and down
motion, mixing each drink
without destroying the
carbonation.

*Yield: 12 servings*

# Bacon Cheese Fingers

*This is an easy and fabulous appetizer Bonnie Bailey and I featured in the luncheon menu prepared for the spring 2002 issue of* Southern Lady *magazine.*

1 cup (4 ounces) shredded
  Swiss cheese
8 slices bacon, crisp-cooked,
  crumbled
1/4 cup mayonnaise
1 tablespoon grated onion
1/2 teaspoon celery salt
1 loaf sliced sandwich bread,
  crusts removed

Mix the cheese, bacon, mayonnaise, onion and celery salt in a medium bowl. Spread the mixture evenly over the bread slices. Arrange on a parchment paper-lined baking sheet. Bake at 325 degrees for 10 minutes. Cut the bread into triangles or other desired shapes before or after baking. To freeze before baking, cut each bread slice into three equal "fingers." Spread 1 tablespoon of the bacon mixture over each finger. Arrange on a baking sheet. Freeze until firm. Place the fingers in a sealable plastic freezer bag and freeze. Bake as directed above, adding a few minutes to the bake time.

*Yield: 12 servings*

# Dilled Squash Soup

*I like to serve this soup along with Bacon Cheese Fingers (above) before family or guests come to the buffet table and while we are still mingling in the family room.*

2 small leeks, sliced
2 tablespoons vegetable oil
1 1/2 pounds yellow squash,
  sliced
3 cups chicken broth
1 cup half-and-half
1 cup sour cream
1/2 to 3/4 teaspoon salt
2 tablespoon minced fresh
  dillweed

Sauté the leeks in the oil in a Dutch oven over medium-high heat until tender. Add the squash and broth and mix well. Bring to a boil; reduce the heat. Simmer, covered, for 8 to 10 minutes or until the squash is tender, stirring occasionally. Remove from the heat to cool slightly. Process the mixture in batches in a food processor until smooth, stopping occasionally to scrape down the side. Pour the soup into a storage container. Stir in the half-and-half, sour cream, salt and dillweed. Chill, covered, for 3 hours or up to 2 days. Pour into a serving bowl. Garnish with sprigs of fresh dillweed.

*Yield: 9 cups*

# Baby Bleu Salad

1 pound mixed salad greens
Balsamic Vinaigrette (below)
4 ounces bleu cheese,
   crumbled
2 oranges, peeled, thinly
   sliced
1 pint fresh strawberries,
   quartered
Sweet-and-Spicy Pecans
   (below)

Toss the salad greens with Balsamic Vinaigrette and the cheese in a large salad bowl. Arrange the orange slices over the greens. Sprinkle with the strawberries and top with Sweet-and-Spicy Pecans.

*Yield: 8 servings*

## Mint Tea

2 (quart-size) tea bags
1 cup sugar
3/4 cup packed fresh mint
   leaves
Juice of 2 lemons
1 quart boiling water
1 quart cold water

Combine the tea bags, sugar, mint leaves and lemon juice in a saucepan. Pour the boiling water over the tea mixture. Steep, covered, for 5 to 10 minutes or until of the desired strength. Remove and discard the tea bags and mint leaves. Pour the mixture into a pitcher. Add the cold water and mix well. Serve over ice in glasses. Garnish with sprigs of fresh mint.

*Yield: 2 quarts*

# Balsamic Vinaigrette

1/2 cup balsamic vinegar
3 tablespoons Dijon mustard
3 tablespoons honey
2 garlic cloves, minced
2 small shallots, minced
1/4 teaspoon salt
1/4 teaspoon pepper
1 cup olive oil

Whisk the vinegar, Dijon mustard, honey, garlic, shallots, salt and pepper together in a medium bowl. Add the olive oil in a fine stream, whisking constantly.

# Sweet-and-Spicy Pecans

1/4 cup sugar
1 cup warm water
1 cup pecan halves
2 tablespoons sugar
1 tablespoon chili powder
1/8 teaspoon ground
   red pepper

Combine 1/4 cup sugar and the water in a medium bowl and stir until the sugar dissolves. Add the pecans and let stand for 10 minutes. Drain the pecans, discarding the syrup. Combine 2 tablespoons sugar, the chili powder and red pepper in a small bowl and mix well. Add the pecans, tossing to coat. Spread the pecan mixture on a lightly greased baking sheet. Bake at 350 degrees for 10 minutes, stirring once.

*Luncheons*

# French Lasagna

8 ounces lasagna noodles
3 quarts boiling water
2 tablespoons olive oil or butter
1 cup chopped onion
4 garlic cloves, minced
1 teaspoon basil
1 teaspoon tarragon
2 cups sliced mushrooms
2 cups ricotta cheese
16 ounces small curd cottage cheese
4 eggs, lightly beaten
3 cups packed chopped fresh spinach
1/4 teaspoon salt
1/4 teaspoon freshly ground pepper
1/4 teaspoon nutmeg
1/2 cup grated Parmesan cheese
1 1/2 cups (6 ounces) shredded mozzarella cheese
Béchamel Sauce (below)

Cook the lasagna noodles in the water in a 4-quart stockpot until al dente; drain. Fill the stockpot with cold water. Place the noodles in the cold water and set aside. Heat the olive oil in a 10-inch skillet over medium heat. Add the onion, garlic, basil and tarragon and sauté until the onion begins to brown. Add the mushrooms and cook until tender, stirring frequently. Combine the ricotta cheese, cottage cheese, eggs, mushroom mixture, spinach, salt, pepper, nutmeg, Parmesan cheese and 1/2 cup of the mozzarella cheese in a large bowl and mix well. Brush a small amount of Béchamel Sauce over the bottom of a 9×12-inch baking dish to cover. Drain the lasagna noodles. Arrange 1/3 of the lasagna noodles in the bottom of the dish. Layer with the cheese mixture and remaining noodles 1/2 at a time. Top with the remaining Béchamel Sauce. Sprinkle evenly with the remaining mozzarella cheese. Bake, covered, at 375 degrees for 30 minutes. Let stand for 10 minutes before serving. No-cook noodles may be used.

*Yield: 6 to 8 servings*

# Béchamel Sauce

1/4 cup (1/2 stick) butter
1/4 cup unbleached white flour
1 3/4 cups milk
1/2 cup grated Parmesan cheese
1/8 teaspoon salt
Pepper to taste

Melt the butter in a 2-quart saucepan or 10-inch cast-iron skillet. Add the unbleached white flour and cook over low heat for a few minutes, stirring constantly. Add the milk gradually, stirring constantly. Add the cheese, salt and pepper. Cook until the sauce thickens, stirring constantly. Thin the sauce with additional milk if necessary. Remove from the heat.

# Cinnamon Chocolate Brownies with Chocolate Ganache

1/2 cup flour

1 1/2 teaspoons cinnamon

1/8 teaspoon salt

6 ounces semisweet chocolate, chopped

3/4 cup (1 1/2 sticks) unsalted butter, chopped, softened

4 eggs

1 cup sugar

1 1/2 teaspoons vanilla extract

1 cup chopped walnuts

2 cups (12 ounces) chocolate chips

1 cup whipping cream

Combine the flour, cinnamon and salt in a small bowl and mix well. Combine 6 ounces chopped chocolate and the butter in the top of a double boiler or microwave for 2 minutes. Stir over simmering water until melted and smooth. Turn off the heat; let stand. Beat the eggs and sugar in a large mixing bowl for 5 minutes or until the mixture thickens and falls in soft ribbons when the beaters are lifted. Beat in the vanilla. Stir in the flour mixture 1/2 at a time, blending well after each addition. Add the warm chocolate mixture gradually, beating just until combined. Stir in the walnuts. Pour into a generously buttered and lightly floured 8×8-inch metal baking pan. Bake on the center oven rack at 350 degrees for 35 minutes or until the top is set and a tester inserted in the center comes out with moist crumbs attached. Cool completely in the pan on a wire rack. Microwave the chocolate chips in a 2-quart microwave-safe bowl until melted. Add the whipping cream and whisk until smooth. Pour evenly over the cooled brownies. Chill, covered, for 2 hours or until the ganache is set. Cut into squares.

*Yield: 16 squares*

*How yummy! My cooking classes have been amazed to find out that the vanilla bean comes from an orchid plant. There are 25,000 varieties of orchids and this one variety, a celadon-colored orchid, is the only one that produces anything edible, the vanilla bean.*

# A Book Club Luncheon

Book clubs are very popular with all ages. Our good friends from Memphis, Mackie and Jim Gibb Johnson, belong to a couple's book club that meets at night. They have dessert and coffee after reviewing their book. Many groups review a book and then enjoy lunch together. Our menu here is easily prepared ahead. Use a centerpiece on your table of books opened at different angles with a blooming plant and a magnifying glass. Of course, if you prefer, you can always serve coffee and cake or muffins in the morning (as "My Little Book Club" does) and conclude before lunch or ask everyone to join you at the club or a local restaurant. If you choose this menu, it would be nice with plates served from the kitchen or as a buffet for your guests. Absolutely everything on this menu can be prepared ahead. The Celebration Punch, Spiced Fresh Fruit, or Cranberry Apple Compote may be whipped up the day before and refrigerated. The Artichoke and Swiss Shortcake could be prepared a day ahead, refrigerated, and reheated. Or you could prepare the shortbread, cook the chicken, and make Plantation Cream Sauce early the morning of your club gathering. Pear muffins and carrots may be made the day before, refrigerated, and reheated. The dessert, the Raspberry Cream Tart, can be made the day before and refrigerated. Let it come to room temperature before serving. Add a mint leaf to the dessert plate. If things get too hectic, buy a dessert and muffins at a special bakery.

# Celebration Punch

8 cups cranapple juice
8 cups pineapple juice
1$^1$/2 cups sugar
2 tablespoons almond extract
2 quarts ginger ale, chilled

Combine the cranapple juice, pineapple juice, sugar and almond extract in a large punch bowl and stir until the sugar dissolves. Add the ginger ale just before serving and stir to mix. Serve in stemmed glasses.

*Yield: 1 gallon*

# Spiced Fresh Fruit

*This is yummy and so easy.*

$^1$/2 cup white wine
$^1$/2 cup honey
$^1$/2 teaspoon cinnamon
$^1$/4 teaspoon allspice
3 tablespoons amaretto
4 cups mixed fresh fruit
   such as raspberries,
   strawberries, orange
   sections, melon balls,
   kiwifruit, peach slices or
   pear slices
3 tablespoons chopped
   fresh mint

Combine the wine, honey, cinnamon, allspice and amaretto in a small bowl and mix well. Combine the fruit in a large bowl and toss gently. Pour the wine mixture over the fruit. Chill, covered, for several hours. Sprinkle with the mint.

*Yield: 4 servings*

# Artichoke and Swiss Shortcake

1 (10-ounce) package corn bread mix
1 (8-ounce) can cream-style corn
1 1/2 cups (6 ounces) shredded natural Swiss cheese
2 eggs, lightly beaten
2 tablespoons milk
2 teaspoons prepared mustard
1 (14-ounce) can artichoke hearts, drained, chopped
1 (3-ounce) can chopped mushrooms, drained
Plantation Cream Sauce (below)

Combine the corn bread mix, corn, 1/2 cup of the cheese, the eggs, milk and prepared mustard in a medium bowl and mix well. Spread 1 cup of the batter in a greased 8×8-inch baking dish. Combine the artichokes, mushrooms and remaining cheese in a medium bowl and mix well. Spoon over the batter in the prepared dish. Top with the remaining batter. Bake at 350 degrees for 35 minutes or until the corn bread is golden brown and has pulled away from the sides of the dish. Let stand for 10 minutes before cutting into squares. Spoon Plantation Cream Sauce over each serving.

*Yield: 6 to 8 servings*

*The Artichoke and Swiss Shortcake with Plantation Cream Sauce was featured in a cooking class that I held for Alabama Legislators' wives touring Decatur.*

# Plantation Cream Sauce

2 tablespoons unsalted butter
2 tablespoons flour
3/4 cup chicken broth
3/4 cup half-and-half
2 egg yolks, lightly beaten
1 cup chopped cooked chicken or turkey
1 cup chopped cooked ham
Salt and pepper to taste

Melt the butter in a medium saucepan. Blend in the flour. Add the broth and half-and-half. Cook over medium-high heat until the sauce thickens and bubbles, stirring constantly. Stir 3/4 cup of the sauce into the egg yolks in a bowl. Pour the egg yolk mixture back into the sauce. Stir in the chicken and ham. Cook over medium-high heat until heated through, stirring constantly. Keep warm.

# Carrots, Pistachios and Cointreau

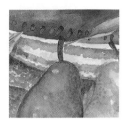

2 pounds carrots, thinly
  sliced in sticks
6 tablespoons water
6 tablespoons butter
1 tablespoon sugar
1 1/2 teaspoons salt
1 cup chopped pistachios
6 tablespoons Cointreau, or
  2 tablespoons frozen
  orange juice concentrate
1 tablespoon grated orange
  zest

Refrigerate the carrots in ice water to cover in a bowl overnight or until the carrots curl slightly at the ends; drain. Place the carrots in a heavy saucepan and add the water, butter, sugar and salt. Bring to a boil quickly, stirring constantly. Reduce the heat to medium-low. Cook, covered, for 5 minutes. Cook, uncovered, for 3 minutes or just until the carrots are tender. The cooking time will vary with the thickness of the carrot slices. Stir the carrot mixture. Remove to a warm serving dish. Add the pistachios, Cointreau and orange zest and mix gently.

*Yield: 6 servings*

# Cranberry Apple Compote

2 cups apple cider
6 tablespoons light corn
  syrup
2 tablespoons packed golden
  brown sugar
1/2 cup (1 stick) unsalted
  butter
3 Golden Delicious apples,
  peeled, cored, cut into
  1/2-inch pieces
2 cups fresh or frozen
  cranberries
1/2 cup (or more) sugar

Whisk the apple cider, corn syrup and brown sugar together in a large heavy saucepan. Boil over high heat for 15 minutes or until reduced to 1 cup. Add 1/2 of the butter and whisk until melted. Remove from the heat. Melt the remaining butter in a large heavy skillet over medium heat. Add the apples and sauté for 2 minutes. Add the cranberries and 1/2 cup of the sugar. Cook for 2 minutes or until the cranberries begin to pop, stirring constantly. Stir in the cider mixture. Boil for 6 minutes or until the mixture is reduced to a syrup consistency, stirring constantly. Stir in additional sugar if desired. Remove to a compote bowl and serve warm.

*Yield: 6 cups*

# Pear Walnut Muffins

2 1/3 cups flour
2 teaspoons baking powder
1/2 teaspoon baking soda
1 cup sugar
1/4 teaspoon salt
1 teaspoon cinnamon
1 teaspoon cardamom
　(optional)
2 small eggs
3/4 cup milk
3/4 cup (1 1/2 sticks) butter,
　melted, cooled
1 cup coarsely chopped
　peeled ripe pear
1/2 cup coarsely chopped
　walnuts
1/2 cup packed light brown
　sugar
1/2 teaspoon cinnamon
1/2 teaspoon cardamom
1/4 cup (1/2 stick) cold butter,
　cut into small pieces

Combine the flour, baking powder, baking soda, sugar, salt, 1 teaspoon cinnamon and 1 teaspoon cardamom in a large bowl and mix well. Add the eggs, milk and melted butter. Stir with a wooden spoon just until combined; do not overbeat. A few lumps in the batter are fine. Stir in the pear and walnuts. Spoon the mixture into 12 paper-lined muffin cups. Combine the brown sugar, 1/2 teaspoon cinnamon, 1/2 teaspoon cardamom and the cold butter in a small bowl and mix with both hands until the topping is crumbly. Scatter the topping evenly over the batter in the muffin cups. Bake at 400 degrees for 20 to 25 minutes or until a wooden pick inserted in the center of 1 of the muffins comes out clean. Serve warm or at room temperature.

*Yield: 1 dozen*

# Frozen Delight

*This is such a quick dessert and does not need anything else served with it.
My friend Jan Worthy shared this recipe with me.*

1/2 gallon vanilla ice cream,
  softened
1/2 gallon chocolate ice
  cream, softened
1 cup strong brewed coffee,
  room temperature
1/2 cup brandy
1/2 cup crème de cacao

Combine the vanilla ice cream, chocolate ice cream, coffee, brandy and crème de cacao in a large bowl and mix well. Pour into a freezer container and freeze for 24 hours. Serve in champagne glasses.

*Yield: 16 servings*

# Raspberry Cream Tart

*This recipe was given to me by my good Georgia friend, Elizabeth
Morrison Pilgrim, commonly known as Liz.*

1 (1-crust) pie pastry
1 1/2 cups fresh raspberries
6 tablespoons sugar
2 eggs
1/2 cup ground blanched
  almonds
3/4 cup confectioners' sugar
1 cup heavy cream

Line a 9-inch straight-sided French tart pan or flan ring with the pastry. Prick the pastry all over with a fork. Bake at 425 degrees until partially baked. Cool on a wire rack. Reduce the oven temperature to 350 degrees. Combine the raspberries and sugar in a small bowl and mix gently. Spread in a single layer in the pie shell. Combine the eggs, almonds, confectioners' sugar and cream in a bowl and beat until thick. Pour over the raspberry mixture. Bake at 350 degrees for 30 minutes or until the top is golden brown. Cool completely on a wire rack before serving.

*Yield: 6 to 8 servings*

# Remembering Johnston Street Cafe Luncheon

*Skinny Soup*
*Johnston Street Chicken Salad*
*Honey Wheat Bread • Turkey Deluxe Sandwich*
*Boursin Cheese Spread*
*Chocolate Raspberry Truffle Cheesecake*
*Sand Tarts*

If you ever heard of my Johnston Street Cafe, I'm sure you heard about the chicken salad, garlic pickles, Turkey Deluxe Sandwich, and the banana bread sandwich among other things. The Skinny Soup was pretty popular, too. People would get so mad if we were out of pickles. We made these pickles and it was hard to keep up with the demands. I included the pickle recipe in *Southern Scrumptious How to Cater Your Own Party* (page 151). I owned Johnston Street Cafe from 1986 to 1997. What an adventure! The chocolate truffle cheesecake, the carrot cake, trifles, roulages, and lemon tarts were always in the dessert case. Try the whole wheat bread recipe. We made six huge loaves every morning. Barbara Griffin, a super cook, made most of the bread. Edwina Jones made all of our good southern corn bread. We had a hot entrée served each day, along with a variety of salads, sandwiches, and homemade desserts. There was a cooler and a freezer out front, packed with take-out items for our customers' future meals. We had a retail section for gourmet gifts and baskets. Catering large events was a big part of the business. Many friends assisted me at Johnston Street Cafe. They were always ready to come down at a moment's notice and chop or mix. Some of these friends were Pat Owens, Jo Hosey, Sybil Crane, Marie Thomas, Jackie Guice, Joyce Nabors, Amanda Littrell, and others. Annie Pearl and James Tapscott helped me to find extra waiters and waitresses for big events. They were wonderful to work with.

# Skinny Soup

2 cups chopped okra
2 (16-ounce) packages frozen
   oriental or stir-fry
   vegetables
1 (28-ounce) can diced
   tomatoes
4 quarts (or more) chicken
   stock or broth
1 teaspoon basil
2 teaspoons thyme
Salt and pepper to taste

Combine the okra, oriental vegetables (without seasoning packets), tomatoes, stock, basil, thyme, salt and pepper in a stockpot. Bring to a boil; reduce the heat. Simmer for 45 minutes, stirring occasionally and adding additional stock if necessary. Add potatoes to the soup for a less carbohydrate-conscious version.

*Yield: 5 to 6 quarts*

# Johnston Street Chicken Salad

*The secret is the very tender chicken and the white pepper.*

3 pounds boneless chicken
   tenders
1 medium onion
1 rib celery
1 carrot
1 tablespoon salt
3 cups chopped celery
2 cups mayonnaise
1 teaspoon white pepper
1/8 teaspoon cayenne pepper
Salt to taste

Rinse the chicken. Combine the chicken, onion, 1 rib celery, carrot and 1 tablespoon salt in water to cover in a large stockpot. Bring to a boil. Cook for 10 minutes from the boiling point. Drain the chicken, discarding the vegetables and reserving the cooking liquid for another use. Cool. Chop the chicken. Combine the chicken, 3 cups celery, the mayonnaise, white pepper, cayenne pepper and salt to taste in a large bowl and mix well. Chill, covered, until serving time.

*Yield: 8 to 10 servings*

*The sign in the entrance of the Johnston Street Cafe dining room expressed our attitude, "Laughter is the Best Medicine." There was plenty of laughter coming out of that kitchen.*

# Honey Wheat Bread

2 envelopes dry yeast
1³/4 cups warm water
   (105 to 115 degrees)
1/4 cup packed light brown
   sugar
1 teaspoon salt
1/2 cup honey
1/4 cup corn oil
3 cups whole wheat flour
1/2 cup cracked wheat
   (optional)
3 to 3¹/2 cups bread flour

Dissolve the yeast in the water in a large bowl. Add the brown sugar, salt, honey and corn oil and mix well. Stir in the whole wheat flour, cracked wheat and 2 cups of the bread flour. Mix, using an electric mixer with a dough hook attachment, for 10 minutes, adding enough of the remaining bread flour to make a dough that holds its shape. Place the dough in a greased bowl, turning to coat the surface. Let rise, covered, in a warm place for 1 to 2 hours or until doubled in bulk. Punch the dough down. Knead gently. Let stand for 15 minutes. Shape gently. Let stand for 15 minutes longer. Shape into 2 equal loaves. Place in 2 well-greased 4×8-inch loaf pans. Let rise, covered, for 1 hour or until doubled in bulk. Bake at 350 degrees for 45 to 60 minutes or until bread tests done. Remove from the pans. Cool on a wire rack.

*Yield: 2 loaves*

# Boursin Cheese Spread

*This is so good spread on each side of a split, warm croissant
with thinly sliced roast beef and a lettuce leaf.*

8 ounces cream cheese,
   softened
2 tablespoons butter,
   softened
2 tablespoons chopped
   parsley
1 tablespoon chives
1/2 teaspoon pressed garlic
1/4 teaspoon dried dillweed
1/8 teaspoon thyme
Cracked black pepper

Process the cream cheese, butter, parsley,
chives, garlic, dillweed, thyme and pepper in
a food processor until blended. Chill, covered,
until ready to use.

*Yield: 3/4 cup*

# Turkey Deluxe Sandwich

*Our most popular sandwich. A real winner.*

2 slices whole wheat
   sandwich bread
2 slices bacon, crisp-cooked,
   drained
2 1/2 ounces sliced cooked
   turkey
2 ounces sliced Swiss cheese
1/4 cup (or less) sprouts
2 slices tomato
Thousand Island salad
   dressing

Grill the bread on both sides. Layer the bacon,
turkey, cheese, sprouts and tomato on 1 slice
of the bread on a microwave-safe plate.
Microwave for 30 seconds. Spread salad
dressing on 1 side of the remaining bread slice
and close to make a sandwich. Cut in half.

*Yield: 1 sandwich*

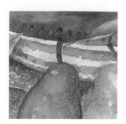

# Chocolate Raspberry Truffle Cheesecake

*This is, without a doubt, one of the best desserts ever. It may be prepared ahead and frozen. Barbara Griffin made hundreds of these for Johnston Street Cafe.*

1¹/2 cups crushed Oreo
   cookies
2 tablespoons butter or
   margarine, melted
Cream Cheese Filling
   (below)
Chocolate Truffles (below)
Chocolate Glaze (below)

Combine the cookie crumbs and butter in a small bowl and mix well. Press over the bottom of a 9-inch springform pan. Pour the Cream Cheese Filling into the prepared pan. Drop Chocolate Truffles by rounded tablespoonfuls over the filling; do not swirl. Bake at 325 degrees for 1 hour and 20 minutes. Cool in the pan on a wire rack. Release and remove the side of the pan. Spread Chocolate Glaze over the top of the cheesecake. Refrigerate, covered, until ready to serve.

*Yield: 8 servings*

## Cream Cheese Filling

24 ounces cream cheese,
   softened
1¹/4 cups sugar
3 eggs
1 cup sour cream
1 teaspoon vanilla extract

Beat the cream cheese with the sugar in a mixing bowl on medium speed until well blended. Add the eggs 1 at a time, beating well after each addition. Add the sour cream and vanilla and beat until smooth.

## Chocolate Truffles

1 cup (6 ounces) chocolate
chips, melted
8 ounces cream cheese,
softened
1/3 cup red raspberry
preserves

Combine the melted chocolate, cream cheese
and raspberry preserves in a bowl and mix well.

## Chocolate Glaze

1 cup (6 ounces) chocolate
chips
1/2 cup whipping cream

Microwave the chocolate chips in a microwave-
safe container on Medium for 1 minute. Stir
the chocolate until smooth. Whisk in the
cream until smooth.

*Put fresh red raspberries on top*

## Sand Tarts

4 cups sifted cake flour
1 tablespoon baking powder
1 cup (2 sticks) butter,
softened
2 cups sugar
2 eggs, well beaten
1 egg white, lightly beaten
1 tablespoon sugar

Sift the cake flour and baking powder into
a large bowl. Cream the butter thoroughly
in a large mixing bowl. Add 2 cups sugar
gradually, beating until light and fluffy. Add
the whole eggs and flour mixture and mix
well. Chill, covered, until firm enough to roll.
Roll the dough 1/2 inch thick on a lightly
floured surface. Cut with floured cookie
cutters. Arrange on an ungreased cookie
sheet. Brush with the egg white and sprinkle
with 1 tablespoon sugar. Bake at 375 degrees
for 10 minutes. Cool on a wire rack.

*Yield: 6 dozen*

*A cookie from my
childhood. My mother was
one of the best cooks ever.
I truly have never eaten a
better sugar cookie. For
years at Johnston Street
Cafe, we made these
cookies for each holiday
and decorated them
appropriately. This is a
recipe you should use and
use. Our grandchildren
love these cookies!*

# Bridesmaids' Luncheon

*Passion Fruit Mimosas*
*Kir Royales*
*Hot Crab Crisps*
*Chicken Crepes with Asparagus and Mushrooms*
*Fruit Salad over a Chiffonade of Romaine with*
*Mango Cream Dressing*
*Citrus Tart from Menton  •  Rolls and Butter*

A Bridesmaids' Luncheon is so exciting in many ways. I always love hosting one since you realize what a special day this is for the bride. I once hosted a bridesmaids' luncheon and the bride became ill and never made it to the luncheon. Thank goodness she was better by the evening. Usually the bride and her bridesmaids do not have voracious appetites. They are too excited. Have something light. These crepes can be made the day before, stuffed, and refrigerated. Make up the topping and refrigerate. Remove crepes from refrigerator and bake. Topping goes on in the last few minutes before serving. The Mango Cream Dressing may be made a day ahead. It is pretty special to serve the plates from the kitchen. Generally, there are not great numbers of people invited to a bridesmaids' luncheon. Recently, I attended a bridesmaids' luncheon at the Old State Bank building, constructed in 1832. What a lovely setting for a luncheon for a lovely girl, Caroline Norman. Caroline worked for me at Johnston Street Cafe as a teenager and now is a grown lady, teaching school, and married.

# Passion Fruit Mimosas

5 cups fresh passion fruit
   juice or passion fruit
   blend nectar
5 cups Champagne, chilled
10 tablespoons Grand
   Marnier

Divide the passion fruit juice evenly among
10 Champagne flutes or saucers. Pour 1/2 cup
Champagne slowly into each flute. Add
1 tablespoon Grand Marnier to each flute.
Garnish with orange twists.

*Yield: 10 servings*

# Hot Crab Crisps

1 cup mayonnaise
1/2 cup finely chopped
   scallions
1 cup freshly grated
   Parmesan cheese
4 drops of Tabasco sauce
1 tablespoon fresh lemon
   juice
8 ounces fresh crab meat,
   shells removed and flaked
2 French baguettes,
   thinly sliced

Combine the mayonnaise, scallions, cheese,
Tabasco sauce and lemon juice in a bowl and
mix well. Fold in the crab meat. Arrange the
bread slices on a baking sheet. Bake at 300
degrees for 10 minutes or until crisp. Spread
each slice with the crab meat mixture. Bake
at 350 degrees for 15 minutes or until light
brown and bubbly.

*Yield: 50 to 55 crisps*

## Kir Royales

4 teaspoons crème
   de cassis
2 bottles Champagne,
   chilled

Pour 1/2 teaspoon crème
de cassis in each of
8 Champagne glasses.
Fill each glass 2/3 full
with the Champagne.

*Yield: 8 servings*

# Basic Crepes

4 eggs
2 cups flour
1 cup milk
1 cup water
1/4 cup (1/2 stick) butter,
  melted
Pinch of salt
Vegetable oil

Combine the eggs and flour in a large bowl and whisk to blend. Add the milk and water gradually, beating until smooth. Beat in the butter and salt. Let stand, covered, in a cool place or in the refrigerator for 1 hour or longer. Thin the batter with additional milk if necessary. The batter should pour like heavy cream. Heat a crepe pan over medium heat until a drop of water sizzles on contact. Brush lightly with the oil and remove from the heat. Fill a 1/4-cup measure 1/2 full with the batter. Pour into the crepe pan and tilt the pan to swirl the batter evenly over the surface in a thin film. Pour any excess batter back into the bowl. Return the pan to the heat. Cook for 1 minute or until the underside is evenly golden and the crepe moves freely. Turn the crepe over using fingertips or a small spatula. Cook for 30 seconds or until the underside is unevenly speckled brown. Remove to a plate. Repeat with the remaining batter, brushing the pan with additional oil as necessary. Stack up to 8 crepes with waxed-paper dividers. Wrap each cooled stack in plastic wrap and refrigerate for up to 3 days. You may freeze the plastic-wrapped stacks in a sealable plastic freezer bag or container. Bring to room temperature and separate the crepes before using. Reheat, wrapped in foil, (not plastic wrap), in a steamer or in the oven at 300 degrees for 10 minutes.

*Yield: 32 to 36 crepes*

# Chicken Crepes

1/4 cup chopped shallots
1 tablespoon butter
3/4 cup chopped mushrooms
2 cups chopped cooked
   chicken tenders
1/4 cup dry sherry
21/2 cups Velouté Sauce
   (at right)
1 pound thin asparagus,
   trimmed
Salt and pepper to taste
Crepes (at left)
1 egg yolk
5 tablespoons whipping
   cream
1/2 cup Velouté Sauce
   (at right)

Sauté the shallots in the butter in a skillet over medium heat until tender. Add the mushrooms and cook until light brown, stirring constantly. Combine the mushroom mixture, chicken, sherry and 21/2 cups Velouté Sauce in a bowl and mix well. Slice off the tips of the asparagus. Cut enough asparagus spears into 1/4-inch pieces to measure 2 cups. Cook the asparagus tips in boiling salted water to cover in a saucepan until tender-crisp. Drain and plunge into a bowl of ice water. Pat dry with paper towels; set aside. Cook the chopped asparagus spears in boiling salted water to cover until tender-crisp. Drain and plunge into a bowl of ice water; drain. Add to the chicken filling. Season with salt and pepper. Spread 1/4 cup of the chicken filling across the center of the speckled side of 1 crepe and roll into a cylinder. Repeat with the remaining filling and crepes. Arrange the crepes, seam side down, in a buttered baking dish. Bake on the center oven rack at 350 degrees for 15 minutes. Combine the egg yolk, 2 tablespoons of the whipping cream and 1/2 cup Velouté Sauce in a bowl and mix well. Beat the remaining whipping cream in a bowl until soft peaks form. Fold into the yolk mixture. Spoon over the baked crepes. Broil until lightly brown. Heat a small amount of butter in a skillet. Add the reserved asparagus tips, tossing until heated through. Sprinkle over the broiled topping.

*Yield: 10 to 12 servings*

## Velouté Sauce

6 tablespoons unsalted
   butter
1/3 cup flour
11/2 cups half-and-half
11/2 cups chicken broth

Melt butter in a 2-quart saucepan over medium heat. Whisk in the flour. Cook for 2 minutes or until bubbly. Add the half-and-half and broth gradually, whisking constantly. Bring to a boil, whisking constantly. Reduce the heat and simmer gently.

*Yield: 3 cups*

# Fruit Salad over a Chiffonade of Romaine with Mango Cream Dressing

1 mango, peeled, chopped
1¹/2 cups mayonnaise
³/4 cup sour cream
3 tablespoons sugar
1 teaspoon vanilla extract
Fresh romaine leaves
Fresh mixed fruit such as
    raspberries, blueberries,
    sliced melon or sliced
    peaches

Purée the mango in a food processor until smooth. Add the mayonnaise, sour cream, sugar and vanilla and process until smooth. Rinse the romaine and pat dry with paper towels. Stack the romaine and roll into bundles. Cut diagonally across the bundles, shredding the romaine. Place on a serving plate. Top with the fresh fruit and mango dressing.

*Yield: 6 servings*

# Tart Pastry (Pâte Sublime)

6 tablespoons heavy cream,
    chilled
1 egg yolk
2 cups flour
2 tablespoons sugar
1 teaspoon baking powder
¹/2 teaspoon salt
10 tablespoons cold unsalted
    butter, cut into pieces

Beat the heavy cream and egg yolk together in a bowl until smooth. Combine the flour, sugar, baking powder and salt in a food processor and process for 2 to 3 seconds or until mixed. Add the butter and pulse for 8 to 10 seconds or until the mixture resembles coarse oatmeal. Pour the cream mixture slowly through the feed tube, processing constantly until the mixture begins to stick together. Knead briefly on a floured surface. Divide the dough into 2 equal portions. Shape each portion into a flat disk and wrap each tightly in plastic wrap. Chill for 30 minutes or longer before rolling.

*Yield: 1 pound pastry (enough for
two 8- or 9-inch tart shells)*

# Citrus Tart from Menton

1/2 recipe Pâte Sublime
   (page 64)
3 eggs
1 egg yolk
Juice of 3 lemons
Juice of 1 orange
1/2 cup heavy cream
2/3 cup sugar

Line an 8-inch tart pan with removable bottom with the Pâte Sublime pastry. Cover the pastry with parchment paper, taking care to protect the edge. Place pie weights or dried beans in the pastry shell. Bake at 450 degrees for 15 minutes. Cool on a wire rack. Reduce the oven temperature to 350 degrees. Combine the eggs, egg yolk, lemon juice, orange juice, cream and sugar in a bowl and whisk until blended and frothy. Remove the pie weights and parchment paper from the baked tart shell. Fill the tart shell 3/4 full with the filling. Place the tart pan on the center oven rack and spoon the remaining filling into the tart shell to prevent spillage. Bake at 350 degrees, with the oven door ajar, for 35 minutes or until the filling is firm. Check the firmness of the filling by shaking the pan slightly. Cool to lukewarm on a wire rack. Remove from the pan. Cool completely on a wire rack. Garnish with neatly peeled lemon segments or candied orange peel, or a sprig of mint and a dollop of whipped cream.

*Yield: 6 to 8 servings*

*This is one of my favorite recipes that I acquired while in southern France. I am very partial to lemon desserts. I keep lemon curd in my refrigerator at all times. (It will keep three weeks in the refrigerator.) It was good for emergency desserts when I owned Johnston Street Cafe.*

# Dinners & Suppers

# Menus

A Taste of Honey—A Casual Supper Party

A Picnic in the Park    •    A Progressive Supper

Tailgating—the Portable Meal

Company in the Kitchen—A Soup Supper

Sweetheart Dinner    •    The French Connection

A Birthday Dinner

A Traditional Holiday Dinner with a Twist

There is always an occasion to entertain family or friends in your home, formally or informally. Christenings, birthdays, engagements, welcoming a new neighbor, or "just getting the group together" for camaraderie provide a wonderful excuse.

Our family always gathers at our home, Sunshine, in Decatur, Alabama, for holiday celebrations. Our largest gathering is at Easter with an Easter Egg hunt followed by a picnic supper "after the hunt." This usually involves about 150 people. The menu changes each year, but generally we have barbeque, hot dogs with the trimmings, salads, and Easter cookies plus a giant dome cake decorated as an Easter Egg for dessert. Of course, drinks are provided, such as tea, lemonade, and soft drinks.

Another dinner we very much enjoy is the Christmas Dinner, formally served in the dining room with the fine china, silver candlesticks, napkins wrapped with ribbons, and our very best "bibs and tuckers" on. Generally the centerpiece is a collection of crystal angels that we have used for years with crystal candlesticks and cream-colored candles intermingled with a bit of Jackson vine. Collections are always great as a centerpiece and, of course, we love to use Jackson vine on our tables in the South. Since there are seventeen of us in our immediate family and we generally have some friends or "in-laws" such as the Patricks, Hofherrs, Wallaces, or Breuers, there is always a crowd, and I do serve "buffet style." For smaller dinners, we serve "family style," serving at the table, or I serve each plate from the kitchen.

It is quite proper to serve buffet style and have each guest hold his plate if you do not wish to set tables. If you do this, then be sure that you serve a menu that does not require a knife such as a salad, a casserole, bread, and dessert.

On many of our travels, we have had the wonderful opportunity to sit next to very interesting people at dinner. On one occasion in Washington, D.C., we were sitting next to Willard Scott, the renowned weatherman, our speaker. Bill had the opportunity to tell him a weather joke. Keep in mind that if you have a seated dinner that you should give some thought as to who should sit by whom so that everyone will have a comfortable and fun time. Bill was the perfect one to sit by Willard, as they both enjoy sharing jokes. The joke was, "What is the similarity between a Southern redneck divorce and a tornado?… Someone is going to lose a trailer."

Dinners, both informal or "casual" and formal, require some careful planning. Good organization assures you of a smooth evening.

# A Taste of Honey—A Casual Supper Party

*Hot Bacon and Gruyère Spread*
*Garlic Mashed Potatoes with Corn and Saffron*
*Pear and Mesclun Salad with Candied Walnuts*
*Pork Tenderloin with Blueberry Balsamic Sauce*
*Buttermilk Biscuits • Gooey Chocolate Cakes*

This menu was featured when I did a cooking class with my friends, Dr. Ewin Jenkins and his wife, Janet. Ewin presented an excellent program on beekeeping. Several of these recipes have a "Taste of Honey." Our family always has a family reunion during the week of Memorial Day. My sister Catherine's family, the Stainbacks, and my brother Bill's family, the Brandons, along with ours, meet in the Destin area. Catherine and Ray's house is in Seaside, and they have us all down for a dinner, and we reciprocate. I had this menu for "our" night. The balsamic vinaigrette may be made and refrigerated a day or several days ahead. Also, the Candied Walnuts may be prepared three days ahead and stored in an airtight container. Early in the day, make the blueberry sauce. In the middle of the afternoon you may go ahead and cook the pork. Cover with foil and serve at room temperature with warm blueberry sauce. Potatoes may be peeled and cut into chunks and placed in cold water early in the day. You may cook the potatoes and cream or mash them before your guests come. Keep warm by placing over a pot of simmering water. The biscuits may be made in the morning and covered with plastic wrap and refrigerated until an hour before baking. The Gooey Chocolate Cakes may be made earlier in the afternoon and baked while you are enjoying the main course or select a yummy deli dessert to serve. You do not have to make every item on the menu.

# Hot Bacon and Gruyère Spread

*This recipe comes from my good buddy, John Harris, a food expert
and a good-hearted man. This is so yummy and so easy. Use low-fat
cream cheese and mayonnaise if you dare.*

16 ounces cream cheese,
  softened
1 cup mayonnaise
2 cups (8 ounces) shredded
  Gruyère or Swiss cheese
1/2 cup chopped scallions
40 slices bacon, crisp-
  cooked, finely chopped
Finely crushed butter
  crackers

Beat the cream cheese in a bowl until smooth
and fluffy. Add the mayonnaise, Gruyère
cheese, scallions and 1/2 of the bacon and
mix well. Spoon the mixture into a baking
dish and sprinkle with the remaining bacon
and crushed crackers. Bake at 350 degrees
for 15 to 20 minutes or until brown and
bubbly. Serve with wheat crackers, crostini
or other crackers.

*Yield: (about) 4 cups*

*Saffron is a most unique
spice with vivid color and a
strong and medicinal flavor.
The quantity used is an
important choice for the
chef. Saffron comes from
the small purple crocus
(crocus sativus). It is
actually the yellow orange
stigmas from the crocus
and is the world's most
expensive spice.*

# Garlic Mashed Potatoes with Corn and Saffron

4 1/2 teaspoons olive oil
3/4 cup chopped onion
1 cup fresh corn kernels
3 garlic cloves, minced
3/4 cup whipping cream
2 tablespoons butter
1/4 teaspoon saffron threads
  (optional)
1 3/4 pounds russet potatoes,
  peeled, cut into 1-inch
  pieces
Salt and pepper to taste

Heat the olive oil in a heavy medium skillet
over medium heat. Add the onion and sauté
for 3 minutes. Add the corn and garlic. Sauté
over medium heat for 5 minutes or until the
onion is golden brown and the corn is tender.
Add the cream, butter and saffron. Bring to a
boil, stirring constantly. Remove from the heat.
Let stand, covered, for 20 minutes. Cook the
potatoes in boiling salted water to cover in a
large pot for 20 minutes or until tender. Drain
well. Mash the potatoes in a large bowl until
smooth. Stir in the corn mixture. Season
with salt and pepper.

*Yield: 6 servings*

# Pear and Mesclun Salad with Candied Walnuts

1 pound mesclun salad
  greens or mixed salad
  greens
Balsamic Vinaigrette
  (at right)
2 firm ripe pears, halved,
  cored, thinly sliced
  lengthwise
Candied Walnuts (below)

Arrange the mesclun greens on a serving platter. Drizzle with Balsamic Vinaigrette. Arrange the pear slices over the top and sprinkle with Candied Walnuts.

*Yield: 4 to 6 servings*

## Balsamic Vinaigrette

1/2 cup balsamic vinegar
3 tablespoons Dijon
  mustard
1/4 cup honey
2 garlic cloves, minced
2 small shallots, minced
1/4 teaspoon salt
1/4 teaspoon pepper
1 cup olive oil

Whisk the vinegar, Dijon mustard, honey, garlic, shallots, salt and pepper together in a bowl until well mixed. Add the olive oil in a fine stream, whisking constantly until blended. This is a delicious vinaigrette to keep in your refrigerator at all times for quick salads.

## Candied Walnuts

1 cup walnut pieces
  (3 to 4 ounces)
2 tablespoons light corn
  syrup
1 tablespoon sugar
1/2 teaspoon salt
1/4 teaspoon ground black
  pepper
Generous pinch of cayenne
  pepper

Combine the walnuts, corn syrup, sugar, salt, black pepper and cayenne pepper in a bowl and mix well. Spread the mixture on a baking sheet sprayed with nonstick cooking spray. Bake at 325 degrees for 15 minutes or until the walnuts are golden brown and the sugar mixture is bubbling, stirring occasionally to break up any clumps. Cool completely on the baking sheet. May be prepared 3 days ahead. Store in an airtight container.

# Pork Tenderloin with Blueberry Balsamic Sauce

2 1/2 cups fresh or frozen
   blueberries
2 tablespoons chopped fresh
   rosemary, or 1 tablespoon
   dried rosemary
2 tablespoons chopped fresh
   thyme, or 1 tablespoon
   dried thyme
1/4 cup balsamic vinegar
1/4 cup honey
2 cups water
1 teaspoon minced garlic
1/2 teaspoon salt
1/2 teaspoon freshly ground
   pepper
1 teaspoon cinnamon
2 tablespoons cornstarch
1/2 cup cold water
3 pounds pork tenderloin
Salt to taste
1/2 cup honey-cup mustard

Combine 2 cups of the blueberries, the rosemary, thyme, vinegar, honey, 2 cups water, the garlic, 1/2 teaspoon salt, the pepper and cinnamon in a medium saucepan and stir gently. Bring to a boil over medium-high heat, stirring constantly. Reduce the heat and simmer for 10 minutes or until the blueberries are tender. Strain the mixture through a fine sieve, discarding the solids. Return the liquid to the saucepan. Dissolve the cornstarch in 1/2 cup cold water in a small cup. Add to the strained liquid. Cook until the liquid is thickened, stirring frequently. Remove from the heat. Stir in the remaining 1 cup blueberries. Rinse the pork and pat dry with paper towels. Arrange the pork on a foil-lined baking sheet and sprinkle with salt. Bake at 325 degrees for 30 minutes. Brush with the honey-cup mustard. Bake for 30 minutes longer or to an internal temperature of 145 degrees on a meat thermometer. Serve with the blueberry sauce on the side or slice the pork and drizzle with the blueberry sauce.

*Yield: 8 to 10 servings*

# Buttermilk Biscuits

2 cups flour
3 1/4 teaspoons baking powder
1 teaspoon sugar (optional)
1/2 teaspoon baking soda
1/2 teaspoon salt
5 tablespoons butter, cut into 1/2-inch pieces
3/4 cup plus 2 tablespoons buttermilk

Combine the flour, baking powder, sugar, baking soda and salt in a food processor and process until mixed. Add the butter and pulse until the mixture resembles coarse meal. Remove to a bowl. Add the buttermilk and stir until the mixture forms a ball. Knead, folding the dough over on itself 5 times, on a lightly floured surface. Pat the dough into an 8-inch square. Cut with a 2 1/2-inch round biscuit cutter. Roll the dough scraps and cut out additional biscuits. Arrange on a nonstick baking sheet. Bake in the center of the oven at 450 degrees for 8 minutes or until golden brown. Serve hot with a taste of honey.

*Yield: about 1 dozen*

# Gooey Chocolate Cakes

5 ounces semisweet chocolate chips
10 tablespoons (1 1/4 sticks) unsalted butter
3 eggs
3 egg yolks
1 1/2 cups confectioners' sugar
1/2 cup flour
Chocolate Sauce (at right)

Melt the chocolate chips and butter in a heavy medium saucepan over low heat, stirring constantly. Cool slightly. Combine the eggs and egg yolks in a large bowl and whisk to blend. Whisk in the confectioners' sugar, chocolate mixture and flour. Divide the batter evenly among 6 buttered 3/4-cup soufflé dishes or custard cups. Arrange the soufflé dishes on a baking sheet. Bake at 450 degrees for 11 minutes or until the edges are set but the centers remain soft and runny. Run a knife around the edge of each cake to loosen. Invert the cakes onto individual dessert plates. Spoon Chocolate Sauce around the base of each cake and serve with ice cream if desired.

*Yield: 6 servings*

## Chocolate Sauce

4 1/2 ounces semisweet chocolate chips
2 ounces unsweetened chocolate, chopped
1/3 cup hot water
1/4 cup light corn syrup
1 teaspoon vanilla extract

Combine the semisweet chocolate, unsweetened chocolate, hot water, corn syrup and vanilla in a microwave-safe container and stir to mix. Microwave on Medium-High for 2 minutes or until the chocolate is very hot. Whisk the mixture until smooth.

# A Picnic in the Park

*White Sangria*
*Bruschetta with Garlic White Bean Topping*
*Cold Asparagus with Sesame-Ginger Vinaigrette*
*Raspberry Spinach*
*Parmesan Chicken or Southern Pecan Chicken*
*Assorted Fruit with Cinnamon Dip*
*Bishop's Bread • Refrigerator Cookies*

A picnic, regardless of the occasion, always makes the day or night a bit more memorable and festive. Food tastes better when eaten outside. It was in the 14th century that some of the earliest picnics are known, and they most likely were connected to medieval hunting feasts. A picnic holds out the promise of effortless entertaining. Most people love a picnic—perhaps because of the informality, a sense of togetherness, or just because it's an old-fashioned idea. A bouquet of flowers in a watering can lends a feel of bright informality, possibly a quilt for a tablecloth. Garnish your food with cheerful sunflowers. Use candles in hurricane lamps in case you have a breeze. Add a little Jackson vine. We have such wonderful portable containers, or if you prefer to have your picnic on the porch, terrace, or just outside in the yard, use pottery platters and plates instead of paper plates. All of this menu may be prepared ahead. Store the Garlic White Bean Topping separately from the Bruschetta until time to serve. Make the sangria a day ahead except for adding the club soda. Either of the chickens may be prepared the "morning of" your picnic. Spinach salad greens may be washed and stored in a sealable plastic bag the day before and dressing may be made several days before and stored in the refrigerator. Of course, the cookies and Bishop's Bread may be made a couple of days ahead. Picnics are so much fun.

# White Sangria

1/2 orange, thinly sliced
Juice of 1/2 orange
1 lemon, thinly sliced
1 (750-milliliter) bottle
  dry white wine
2 tablespoons sugar
2 tablespoons brandy
2 tablespoons Cointreau
2 cups ice cubes
1 cup club soda

Combine the orange slices, orange juice, lemon slices, wine, sugar, brandy and Cointreau in a decorative pitcher. Chill until serving time. Add the ice and club soda and stir gently.

*Yield: (about) 4 servings*

# Bruschetta with Garlic White Bean Topping

1/3 cup olive oil
1 large garlic clove, peeled,
  split lengthwise
16 (3/4-inch) slices French
  bread
Garlic White Bean Topping
  (at right)

Preheat a broiler for 10 minutes. Warm the olive oil and garlic in a small saucepan over medium heat for 5 minutes. Brush the garlic mixture over both sides of each bread slice. Arrange on a baking sheet. Toast each side under the broiler until light brown. Spoon Garlic White Bean Topping over each slice and serve. Store toasted bruschetta slices in an airtight container until ready to top and serve.

*Yield: 4 servings*

## Garlic White Bean Topping

2/3 cup rinsed drained
  canned cannellini
  beans
1/4 teaspoon finely
  chopped fresh rosemary
Large pinch of crushed
  red pepper
2 1/2 teaspoons extra-
  virgin olive oil
2 small garlic cloves,
  minced
Salt and freshly ground
  black pepper

Combine the beans, rosemary and crushed red pepper in a food processor and process until mixed. Add the olive oil, garlic, salt and black pepper and process until smooth.

# Cold Asparagus with Sesame Ginger Vinaigrette

1 pound fresh asparagus,
  trimmed
Salt to taste
1 tablespoon toasted sesame
  seeds
1 small garlic clove
1 teaspoon grated fresh
  gingerroot
2 tablespoons rice vinegar
2 tablespoons orange juice
2 teaspoons soy sauce
2 tablespoons vegetable oil
1 tablespoon sugar
1 tablespoon hot chili oil
1 tablespoon sesame oil

Cook the asparagus in lightly salted boiling water to cover in a medium skillet for 5 minutes or just until tender-crisp. Drain the asparagus and plunge into ice water to stop the cooking process. Drain and pat dry with paper towels. Arrange the asparagus on a serving platter. Combine the sesame seeds, garlic, gingerroot, vinegar, orange juice, soy sauce, vegetable oil, sugar, chili oil and sesame oil in a blender and blend until thoroughly mixed. Pour the dressing evenly over the asparagus and serve.

*Yield: 4 servings*

## Toasted Sesame Seeds

*To toast sesame seeds, place them in a small skillet and heat just until fragrant and golden brown, stirring frequently and watching carefully to prevent burning.*

# Raspberry Spinach

*This dressing is so simple and so tasty.*

2 tablespoons raspberry jam
2 tablespoons raspberry
  vinegar
1/3 cup vegetable oil
8 cups fresh spinach leaves,
  rinsed, torn
3/4 cup walnut pieces
1 cup fresh raspberries
3 kiwifruit, peeled, sliced

Combine the jam and vinegar in a blender or small bowl and mix well. Add the oil in a fine stream, blending constantly. Combine the dressing with the spinach, 1/2 of the walnuts, 1/2 of the raspberries and 1/2 of the kiwifruit in a bowl and toss gently to coat. Top with the remaining walnuts, raspberries and kiwifruit. Serve immediately.

*Yield: 8 servings*

add: 2 T. orange juice
to dressing
  2 T raspberry jam
  2 T. rasp. vinegar
  2 T. O
  1/3 cup canola oil

# Parmesan Chicken

2 to 4 tablespoons white
    wine
1/2 cup Dijon mustard
1 cup fresh bread crumbs
1 cup grated Parmesan
    cheese
3 pounds boneless chicken
    breasts

Add enough wine to the Dijon mustard in a bowl to make of a dipping consistency, mixing well. Combine the bread crumbs and cheese in a shallow dish and mix well. Dip each chicken piece in the Dijon mustard mixture and roll in the bread crumb mixture to coat. Arrange the chicken pieces on a greased baking sheet. Bake at 375 degrees for 45 minutes or until cooked through. This dish is good served hot or at room temperature and makes a great choice for the picnic basket.

*Yield: 4 to 6 servings*

# Southern Pecan Chicken

2 pounds boneless skinless
    chicken breasts or chicken
    fingers
1 1/2 cups buttermilk
2 cups pecan pieces
1 1/2 cups flour
1 1/2 teaspoons salt
1/2 teaspoon pepper
Canola oil for frying

Cut each chicken breast into 4 equal strips. Place the chicken strips in a bowl and cover with the buttermilk. Marinate, covered, in the refrigerator for 30 minutes. Combine the pecans, flour, salt and pepper in a food processor and pulse until the pecans are coarsely chopped. Remove the mixture to a bowl. Drain the chicken, discarding the buttermilk. Dip each chicken strip in the pecan mixture, pressing to coat. Refrigerate, covered, for 30 minutes. Heat the canola oil in a deep fryer or cast-iron skillet over high heat until very hot. Drop the chicken strips carefully into the hot oil. Cook for 8 minutes, turning once halfway through the cooking time. Drain on paper towels. Serve at room temperature.

*Yield: 6 to 8 servings*

# Assorted Fruit with Cinnamon Dip

1 cup sour cream
1/4 cup packed brown sugar
1/4 teaspoon cinnamon
1 pound seedless green
  grapes, separated into
  small clusters
1 pound seedless red grapes,
  separated into small
  clusters
1 pint fresh blueberries
1 pint fresh raspberries
1 pint dark sweet cherries
1 cantaloupe, peeled, sliced

Combine the sour cream, brown sugar and cinnamon in a bowl and mix well. Arrange the grapes, blueberries, raspberries, cherries and cantaloupe on a serving platter. Serve with the Cinnamon Dip.

*Yield: 10 to 12 servings*

# Bishop's Bread

*This recipe is from the book by my friend, Jackie Guice, When the Knead Rises. Jackie has taken this to many book signings and received rave reviews.*

1 cup flour
1/4 teaspoon salt
3 eggs
1 cup sugar
1 teaspoon almond extract
1 teaspoon grated lemon zest
1 cup chopped dates
1/2 cup chopped toasted almonds
1/2 cup chopped black walnuts
1 cup (6 ounces) chocolate chips

Mix the flour and salt together. Combine the eggs, sugar and almond extract in a medium bowl and beat with an electric mixer until creamy. Add the flour mixture and mix well. Stir in the remaining ingredients. Pour into a well greased 5×9-inch loaf pan or 9-inch round ovenproof serving dish. Bake at 300 degrees for 40 to 50 minutes or until a wooden pick inserted in the center comes out clean. Cool in the pan on a wire rack for 10 minutes. Remove from the pan. Cool completely on a wire rack. Cut into thin slices or small wedges to serve.

*Yield: 1 loaf*

# Refrigerator Cookies

4 cups flour
1 teaspoon baking soda
1 teaspoon cream of tartar
1 teaspoon salt
1/2 cup (1 stick) butter, softened
1/2 cup shortening
2 cups packed brown sugar
2 eggs
1 teaspoon vanilla extract
1 cup chopped pecans

Sift the flour, baking soda, cream of tartar and salt together. Cream the butter, shortening and brown sugar in a large bowl until light and fluffy. Beat in the eggs and vanilla until smooth. Add the dry ingredients and mix well. Stir in the pecans. Shape the dough into 2 rolls, each 2 inches in diameter. Wrap individually in waxed paper or plastic wrap. Refrigerate or freeze until ready to bake. Cut the rolls into slices 1/8 inch thick. Arrange on a nonstick cookie sheet. Bake at 350 degrees for 8 minutes. Cool on a wire rack.

*Yield: 5 dozen*

*These cookies have an excellent flavor and are very crisp. This recipe of my mother's is very dear to my heart as I discovered it written in her handwriting and found myself missing her once again. We kept this cookie dough on hand in our refrigerator for many unexpected guests. The dough freezes well for up to 1 month.*

# A Progressive Supper

*Boursin Cheese and Grilled Veggie Torta*
*Dirty Corn Dip*
*Spinach Salad with Pancetta and Pine Nuts*
*Layered Asparagus and Crab Meat Casserole • Favorite Roast Tenderloin*
*Corn Pie with Roasted Red Peppers and Green Chiles*
*Bread Pudding with Praline Sauce*

The progressive supper eases the burden on you as the primary planner. It takes guests from one house to another on a dining adventure. It begins with appetizers and beverages at the first location, the entrée and salad at the second location, and the sweet finale and coffee bar at the third location. Get together with two friends, think creatively, plan the menu, and assign courses. You might choose a theme such as an International Evening, or Herbs and Flowers, using herbs in clusters with flowers for centerpieces. Send invitations designed with your theme in mind. This is so much fun. You might plan this as a neighborhood venture and walk from house to house or ride together on a bus if locations are a distance apart. Another easy way to entertain a group is the Pot Luck Dinner. The hostess provides the meat and beverages and asks others to bring appetizers, salads, vegetables, bread, and desserts. The guests take "pot luck" on what the actual menu is. When we were in medical school, this was a very economical way to get together and enjoy a meal. This is held at one location. For the couple who is hosting the appetizer party for the progressive supper, the grilled veggie torta can be made a couple of days ahead and refrigerated. Beer and wine or cold drinks may be served. The next "stop" is for the entrée course, which includes the salad that can be tossed together at the last minute. The hostess could slip out a little early from the first house to ready herself for her part. The favorite roast tenderloin can be completed and held at room temperature. A quick warm-up in the microwave just before serving would be in order. The corn pie can be baked at the last minute, but it could be mixed up just before going to the appetizer party. Another thought is to bake breads the morning of the event and rewarm. Dessert and coffee are the sweet finale to a wonderful evening of good food and camaraderie. The bread pudding may actually be made the day before and rewarmed. It's fun not to have the entire responsibility of hosting. Provide a coffee bar or maybe set up an espresso machine. It would be nice to provide a small favor such as an herb plant in a small terra cotta pot with a bow if your theme is Herbs and Flowers.

# Boursin Cheese and Grilled Veggie Torta

2 teaspoons pressed garlic
1/2 cup (1 stick) butter, softened
1/2 teaspoon dill weed
1/2 teaspoon thyme
1/2 cup chopped fresh parsley
1/4 cup chopped fresh chives
32 ounces cream cheese, softened
Cracked pepper to taste
Grilled or roasted vegetables such as red, green and yellow bell peppers and red onions

Process the garlic in a food processor until smooth. Add the butter, dill weed, thyme, parsley, chives, cream cheese and cracked pepper and process until smooth. Layer the Boursin cheese and grilled vegetables alternately in a mold lined with plastic wrap. Refrigerate, covered, until firm. Unmold onto a serving platter and remove the plastic wrap. Garnish with pine nuts and herb sprigs. Serve with pita chips, crostini or Bremner Wafers.

*Yield: 8 to 10 servings*

# Spinach Salad with Pancetta and Pine Nuts

*This salad takes the Italian route with the addition of pancetta, pine nuts or walnuts, and balsamic vinegar.*

3 tablespoons pine nuts or walnuts
4 ounces pancetta or slab bacon, cut into bite-size pieces
3 tablespoons balsamic vinegar
1 teaspoon red wine vinegar
Kosher salt and freshly ground pepper to taste
1/3 cup extra-virgin olive oil
8 cups fresh spinach leaves

Spread the pine nuts on a baking sheet. Toast in the oven at 350 degrees for 3 to 5 minutes or until light brown, watching carefully to prevent burning. Cook the pancetta in a medium skillet over medium heat until crisp. Drain on paper towels. Whisk the balsamic vinegar, red wine vinegar, salt and pepper together in a large salad bowl. Add the olive oil in a fine stream, whisking constantly until blended. Add the spinach and toss gently to coat. Divide evenly among 6 salad plates and sprinkle with the pancetta and pine nuts. Serve immediately.

*Yield: 6 servings*

## Dirty Corn Dip

*Kitty Caddell White shared this recipe with me. Very easy and good for a crowd.*

1 can Ro-Tel tomatoes, drained
16 ounces whipped cream cheese
1 cup chipotle salsa
3/4 cup mayonnaise
2 cups finely shredded Cheddar cheese
2 cans white niblet corn, drained
Corn chips

Combine the tomatoes, cream cheese, salsa, mayonnaise, Cheddar cheese and corn in a bowl and mix well. Serve with the corn chips.

*Yield: 30 servings*

# Layered Asparagus and Crab Meat Casserole

*This recipe would also make a great brunch or lunch dish served with fresh fruit and a muffin.*

14 slices white bread, crusts removed
1 pound lump crab meat, shells removed, flaked
1 cup coarsely chopped steamed fresh asparagus or drained canned asparagus
3 tablespoons chopped scallions
3/4 cup mayonnaise
2 cups (8 ounces) shredded Swiss cheese
1/3 cup grated Parmesan cheese
10 eggs
2 cups milk
1 tablespoon Dijon mustard
1 teaspoon Worcestershire sauce
1 teaspoon salt
1/2 teaspoon freshly ground pepper

Arrange 1/2 of the bread slices in a 3-quart baking dish sprayed with nonstick cooking spray. Combine the crab meat, asparagus, scallions and mayonnaise in a bowl and mix well. Spread over the bread slices in the prepared dish. Combine the Swiss cheese and Parmesan cheese in a bowl and toss to mix. Sprinkle 1/2 of the cheese mixture over the crab meat mixture. Refrigerate the remaining cheese mixture. Top the prepared layers with the remaining bread. Combine the eggs, milk, Dijon mustard, Worcestershire sauce, salt and pepper in a bowl and mix well. Pour over the bread. Refrigerate, covered, for 2 to 12 hours. Remove from the refrigerator 1 hour before baking. Bake at 350 degrees for 30 minutes or until brown and puffed. Sprinkle with the remaining cheese mixture. Bake for 5 to 10 minutes longer or until bubbly.

*Yield: 10 servings*

# Favorite Roast Tenderloin

*This recipe is from my good friend, Julie Vigeland, who lives in Oregon and loves to entertain.*

3 tablespoons lemon juice
2 tablespoons chopped fresh
  chives
1/4 cup dry white wine
1/4 cup port
1 1/2 teaspoons salt
1/2 teaspoon freshly ground
  pepper
2 teaspoons Worcestershire
  sauce
1 (6-pound) beef tenderloin
2 tablespoons water
2 tablespoons butter

Combine the lemon juice, chives, white wine, port, salt, pepper and Worcestershire sauce in a sealable plastic bag. Add the beef and seal the bag. Marinate in the refrigerator overnight. Turn the bag occasionally, the following day, until roasting time. Drain the beef, reserving the marinade. Place the beef on a rack in a roasting pan. Roast at 425 degrees for 45 to 55 minutes or until of desired doneness, basting occasionally with 1/2 of the reserved marinade. Pour the remaining marinade into a small saucepan during the last few minutes of roasting time. Add the water and butter to the saucepan and bring to a rolling boil, stirring constantly. Boil for 1 to 3 minutes, stirring constantly. Slice the beef and spoon the sauce over the top. Garnish with a combination of sautéed fresh and dried mushrooms.

*Yield: 12 to 15 servings*

*For another complete menu that will delight your guests, roast the following with the meat: Small red or Finnish potatoes, diced turnips, and rutabagas. Brush meat and vegetables with marinade while baking. Add to the meal fresh steamed asparagus and a salad of Bibb lettuce, grapefruit, and avocado. Prepare for accolades.*

# Corn Pie with Roasted Red Peppers and Green Chiles

1 (7-ounce) jar roasted red bell peppers, drained

2 (10-ounce) packages frozen corn, thawed

1 cup (2 sticks) unsalted butter, melted

4 eggs, beaten

1 cup yellow cornmeal

2 teaspoons salt

1 cup sour cream (nonfat may be used)

1 cup (4 ounces) shredded Swiss cheese

1 cup (4 ounces) shredded extra-sharp Cheddar cheese

1 (4-ounce) can chopped green chiles

Rinse the bell peppers and pat dry with paper towels. Chop the bell peppers. Blend the corn in a blender at low speed until partially puréed but not smooth. Pour into a large mixing bowl. Add the butter, eggs, cornmeal, salt, sour cream, Swiss cheese, Cheddar cheese, bell peppers and green chiles and mix well. Pour into a greased 10-inch deep-dish pie plate; do not overfill. (Any extra batter may be baked separately in custard cups.) Bake at 375 degrees for 40 to 50 minutes or until golden brown and firm to the touch. You may double the recipe, using three 9-inch pie plates.

*Yield: 8 servings*

# Bread Pudding with Praline Sauce

1¹/2 pounds country-style
　Italian or French bread,
　thinly sliced
5 eggs
3 cups milk
1¹/2 cups sugar
¹/4 teaspoon salt
3 tablespoons vanilla extract
1¹/2 cups raisins
1 cup chopped pecans,
　lightly toasted
3 tablespoons sugar
1 teaspoon cinnamon
¹/2 teaspoon freshly grated
　nutmeg
¹/2 cup (1 stick) butter,
　cut into small pieces
Praline Sauce (at right)

Toast the bread slices lightly and tear into bite-size pieces. Place in a large bowl. Combine the eggs, milk, 1¹/2 cups sugar, the salt and vanilla in a bowl and mix well. Pour over the bread. Let stand until the liquid is completely absorbed. Fold in the raisins and pecans. Pour into a buttered 9×13-inch glass baking dish and smooth the top with a spatula. Combine 3 tablespoons sugar, the cinnamon and nutmeg in a small bowl and mix well. Sprinkle over the bread mixture. Dot with the butter. Set the baking dish, covered with foil, into a larger baking pan. Fill the larger baking pan halfway with hot water. Bake at 350 degrees for 50 to 60 minutes or until firm and a knife inserted in the center comes out clean. Uncover and let stand for 10 minutes. Serve with warm Praline Sauce spooned over the top.

*Yield: 16 servings*

## Praline Sauce

1 cup (2 sticks) unsalted
　butter
1 cup packed brown sugar
1 cup heavy cream

Combine the butter, brown sugar and cream in a saucepan. Bring to a boil over high heat. Cook, stirring constantly, until the butter is melted. Reduce the heat. Simmer for 5 minutes, stirring frequently.

# Tailgating—The Portable Meal

*Lemon Dill Deviled Eggs*
*Deviled Eggs with Curry • Spicy Deviled Eggs*
*Greek Spinach Squares*
*Potato Swiss Salad*
*Corn Salad*
*Grilled Asparagus*
*Barbecued Baby Back Pork Ribs*
*Cheesecake Squares • Glazed Crackers*

Food is the focal part of any great tailgate party. The secret is to select foods that will satisfy everyone's taste and offer something different too. Pork is the perfect choice since it is so versatile. Remember that tailgaters are on their feet, so handheld or fork-only foods are most convenient. Take plenty of brightly colored paper plates and napkins. Decorate with pennants and mums in a galvanized bucket. Take along a thermos of lemonade or tea, and don't forget the cups. Prepare the Greek Spinach Squares as well as the ribs and all of the salads and eggs a day ahead. Cheesecake Squares and Glazed Crackers can be done several days ahead. You may want to put all food items for the tailgate in small containers and present each guest with a lunch box tied with school colors of your favorite team. There are many memories lingering with the Sims of tailgate parties at Auburn. We took some wonderful football weekend trips to Stillwaters, near the Auburn campus, with our friends the Cranes.

*Take your pick of these delicious deviled egg recipes,
all easily transported.*

# Lemon Dill Deviled Eggs

8 hard-cooked eggs
2 tablespoons mayonnaise
2 tablespoons yogurt or
  sour cream
1/2 teaspoon grated
  lemon zest
1 tablespoon dill weed
1 teaspoon finely chopped
  scallions
1/4 teaspoon dry mustard
1/8 teaspoon salt
1/8 teaspoon pepper

Cut the eggs into halves lengthwise. Mash the egg yolks in a bowl. Add the mayonnaise, yogurt, lemon zest, dill weed, scallions, dry mustard, salt and pepper and mix well. Spoon into the egg whites. Arrange on a bed of parsley on a serving platter. Chill, covered, until serving time. Garnish with caviar.

*Yield: 8 servings*

# Deviled Eggs with Curry

8 hard-cooked eggs
1/4 cup plain yogurt or sour
  cream
1/2 teaspoon curry powder
1/2 teaspoon turmeric
1 teaspoon finely chopped
  fresh parsley
1 tablespoon minced
  scallions
1/4 teaspoon salt

Cut the eggs into halves lengthwise. Mash the egg yolks in a bowl. Add the yogurt, curry powder, turmeric, parsley, scallions and salt and mix well. Spoon into the egg whites. Arrange on a serving platter. Garnish with a sprinkling of paprika.

*Yield: 8 servings*

## Spicy Deviled Eggs

8 hard-cooked eggs
1/4 cup plain yogurt or
  sour cream
1 tablespoon prepared
  mustard
1 tablespoon drained
  canned chopped
  green chiles
2 teaspoons finely
  chopped cilantro
1/4 teaspoon salt
1/8 teaspoon cumin
Dash of ground red
  pepper (cayenne)

Cut the eggs into halves lengthwise. Mash the egg yolks in a bowl. Add the yogurt, prepared mustard, green chiles, cilantro, salt, cumin and red pepper and mix well. Spoon into the egg whites. Arrange on a serving platter.

*Yield: 8 servings*

# Greek Spinach Squares

2 tablespoons butter
2 tablespoons flour
$1/2$ teaspoon salt
$1/8$ teaspoon white pepper
1 cup milk
6 tablespoons butter
1 cup chopped yellow onion
2 pounds fresh spinach
$1/2$ teaspoon salt
$1/4$ teaspoon black pepper
6 eggs, beaten
$1^1/2$ cups crumbled feta
  cheese
6 phyllo pastry sheets
6 tablespoons butter,
  melted

Melt 2 tablespoons butter in a small saucepan over low heat. Add the flour, salt and white pepper and stir to blend. Remove from the heat. Stir in the milk gradually and return to the heat. Cook until thick and smooth, stirring constantly; set aside. Melt 6 tablespoons butter in a large Dutch oven over medium heat. Add the onion and spinach and sauté for 20 minutes or until the spinach is tender. Season with the salt and black pepper. Let stand until cool. Combine the eggs, cheese and white sauce in a medium bowl and mix well. Add to the spinach mixture and mix well. Place 1 pastry sheet in a 9×12-inch baking dish. Brush with 1 tablespoon of the melted butter. Spoon $1/6$ of the spinach mixture over the prepared pastry sheet. Repeat the layers until all ingredients are used, ending with a buttered pastry sheet. Bake at 350 degrees for 30 minutes. Cut into squares to serve. This recipe freezes well.

*Yield: 10 to 12 servings*

# Potato Swiss Salad

3 pounds unpeeled small red
   or Ore-gold potatoes
6 hard-cooked eggs, chopped
1/4 cup finely chopped onion
2 1/4 cups mayonnaise
6 tablespoons milk
1 teaspoon salt
1 teaspoon ground pepper
1 cup (4 ounces) shredded
   sharp Cheddar cheese
1 cup (4 ounces) shredded
   Swiss cheese

Boil the potatoes in enough water to cover in a large saucepan just until tender; drain. Cool and cut into quarters. Combine the potatoes, eggs and onion in a bowl and toss to mix. Combine the mayonnaise, milk, salt and pepper in a bowl and mix well. Add to the potato mixture and mix well. Add the Cheddar cheese and Swiss cheese and stir to mix. Chill, covered, until serving time.

*Yield: 10 servings*

# Corn Salad

2 (16-ounce) packages frozen
   Shoe Peg corn, cooked,
   drained
1 green bell pepper, seeded,
   chopped
1 cup sliced cherry tomatoes
   (optional)
1/2 cup chopped purple onion
3/4 cup chopped cucumber
1/2 cup mayonnaise
1/4 cup sour cream
1 tablespoon apple cider
   vinegar
1/2 teaspoon celery salt
1/2 teaspoon white pepper
Salt to taste

Combine the corn, bell pepper, tomatoes, onion and cucumber in a large bowl and toss to mix. Combine the mayonnaise, sour cream, vinegar, celery salt, white pepper and salt in a small bowl and whisk to blend. Pour over the corn mixture and mix well. Refrigerate, covered, for 3 hours or longer.

*Yield: 6 to 8 servings*

*My friend and travel buddy Eydie Swanson, who is a fabulous cook, gave me this recipe. Eydie and I met fourteen years ago at a Martha Stewart seminar in Westport, Connecticut. We found out that both our husbands were orthopaedists, and we've been fast friends ever since. Sybil Crane, a special lady and friend, makes her potato salad with the addition of bacon. Sybil helped me out so much at Johnston Street Cafe. We sold tons of her delicious rolls from the take-out case.*

## Tailgating
## How-To's

*Packing Game Plan—For on-site tailgating, pack food in self-sealing bags and disposable containers. Remember to bring trash bags and disposable hand wipes. Pack extra rain ponchos and umbrellas in case of bad weather.*

*Know the Drill—"Take Five" and familiarize yourself with your stadium tailgating area before game day. If overnight parking is allowed, you may find it easier to stake out a great spot ahead of time and stash nonperishable supplies on-site. Aim for an area away from the stadium for easy access. Parking next to a grassy area or at the end of a parking row will give you more room to spread out and even toss a football around.*

# Grilled Asparagus

*This is the way my good friend Ron Casey grills asparagus.
This transports well.*

**1 pound fresh asparagus, trimmed**
**1 cup soy sauce**
**1/2 cup vegetable oil or olive oil**
**Pepper to taste**

Place the asparagus in a shallow glass dish. Combine the soy sauce, oil and pepper in a small bowl and mix well. Pour over the asparagus. Marinate for 10 to 15 minutes; drain. Arrange the asparagus on a grill rack over hot coals. Grill for 5 to 7 minutes or until done to taste, turning occasionally. Cool and place in a covered container. Serve at room temperature. May be prepared 1 day ahead and refrigerated overnight.

*Yield: 4 to 6 servings*

# Barbecued Baby Back Pork Ribs

8 pounds baby back
  pork ribs
Barbecue Sauce (below)

Parboil the pork ribs in enough water to cover in a stockpot for 15 minutes; drain. Pat the pork ribs dry. Arrange in a foil-lined roasting pan. Bake, covered, at 300 degrees for 2 hours or until cooked through and tender. Cut into serving pieces. Grill over hot coals for 15 to 20 minutes, turning and basting with Barbecue Sauce. Serve with additional Barbecue Sauce at room temperature.

*Yield: 10 servings*

## Barbecue Sauce

2 tablespoons butter
1 small onion, finely
  chopped
1 garlic clove, finely chopped
3 tablespoons lemon juice
1 tablespoon soy sauce
1 tablespoon Worcestershire
  sauce
2 teaspoons hot red pepper
  sauce
3 cups ketchup
1/2 cup packed brown sugar
1/2 cup water

Combine the butter, onion, garlic, lemon juice, soy sauce, Worcestershire sauce, hot red pepper sauce, ketchup, brown sugar and water in a medium saucepan and mix well. Bring to a boil, stirring constantly. Reduce the heat. Simmer until the flavors are blended and the sauce reaches the desired consistency, stirring frequently. May be transported in a covered container.

## Tailgating How-To's

*Get Fired Up*—If you're planning to grill at your tailgate, don't forget to stow several large bottles of water in your vehicle to extinguish charcoal before game time. Some stadiums also offer receptacles to dispose of used charcoal.

*Don't Forget to Decorate*—Decorate your tailgate party with team pennants and balloons. Fly your team flag high so friends can easily locate your vehicle. Remember to bring a portable CD player so you can sing along with your team's fight song.

## Cheesecake Squares

1/3 cup butter, softened
1/3 cup packed brown sugar
1 cup flour
1/2 cup finely chopped
   pecans
8 ounces cream cheese,
   softened
1/4 cup sugar
1 egg
2 tablespoons milk
1 tablespoon lemon juice

Cream the butter and brown sugar in a mixing bowl or food processor until light and fluffy. Add the flour and pecans and mix until crumbly. Reserve 1 cup of the mixture. Press the remaining mixture over the bottom of an 8- or 9-inch square baking pan. Bake at 350 degrees for 12 to 15 minutes or until light brown. Combine the cream cheese and sugar in a bowl and blend until smooth. Add the egg, milk and lemon juice and beat until smooth. Spread over the baked crust. Sprinkle evenly with the reserved pecan mixture. Bake at 350 degrees for 20 to 25 minutes or until the dessert tests done. Cool on a wire rack. Cut into squares.

*Yield: (about) 1 dozen*

*This recipe for Cheesecake Squares is Katherine Wilks' recipe. Katherine and I edited the first Cotton Country Cooking 26 years ago and have a lifetime friendship as a result. These are so yummy. My sister, Catherine, loves this recipe too.*

## Glazed Crackers

*You'll swear you've made a big mess while these are baking and bubbling, but they turn out so good! "Try these!" says Peggy Burkhart, my buddy from Kentucky.*

1/2 cup (1 stick) unsalted
   butter
1/2 cup (1 stick) margarine
1/2 cup sugar
1 cup confectioners' sugar
1 teaspoon vanilla extract
1 cup chopped pecans
2 packages butter crackers
   (8 ounces)

Combine the butter, margarine, sugar and confectioners' sugar in a saucepan. Bring to a boil. Cook until the butter and margarine melt, stirring constantly. Boil for 3 minutes, stirring constantly. Remove from the heat. Add the vanilla and pecans and mix well. Arrange the crackers on a baking sheet and spoon the butter mixture over the top. Bake at 325 degrees for 8 minutes. Remove from the oven and cool on the baking sheet for 1 minute. Remove to a wire rack to cool completely. Store in an airtight container.

*Yield: 72 crackers*

# Company in the Kitchen—A Soup Supper

*Crostini with Roasted Garlic and Apple Chutney*
*New England Clam Chowder*
*Courtland Chicken Stew*
*A Salad Medley  •  Herbed Muffins*
*Chocolate Trifle with Black Cherries and Pears*

The kitchen is the heart of many a home so it's no surprise we love entertaining there. A soup buffet is one of the easiest, most versatile, and least expensive ways to entertain groups of friends or family, from four to forty. Particularly in the winter months, soups are warm and welcoming. They can all be made ahead. The Crostini can be made ahead, the garlic roasted, and the Apple Chutney made as far as a week ahead. I have some small round deep soup bowls that I like to use since they fit on a dinner plate nicely, leaving room for breads and salad. In the basement of my home, I have a commercial, entertaining kitchen where I teach cooking classes. I love it! I am like the "mad scientist" in my laboratory. I built this kitchen when I sold Johnston Street Cafe. This is a perfect place for a soup supper. Both the soups in this menu may be made a day ahead, as may the trifle. That leaves only the salad and the Herbed Muffins to do the "day of."

# Crostini with Roasted Garlic and Apple Chutney

*You could substitute "store bought" mango chutney if you didn't have the time to make apple. The apple chutney could be made a week ahead or months if you processed it or "canned" it.*

## Roasted Garlic

4 large garlic bulbs
1/4 cup olive oil
Salt and pepper

Slice 1/4 inch off the tops of the garlic bulbs, exposing the cloves. Place the garlic in a small baking dish. Drizzle with the oil and sprinkle with salt and pepper, tossing to coat. Turn the garlic cut side up. Roast, covered tightly with foil, at 350 degrees for 55 minutes or until the garlic skins are golden brown and the garlic cloves are tender. Cool on a wire rack. Squeeze each garlic clove to release the skin.

1 cup packed golden brown
   sugar
3/4 cup rice vinegar
2 garlic cloves, minced
11/2 teaspoons minced fresh
   gingerroot
1/8 teaspoon cayenne pepper
1 cinnamon stick
11/2 pounds Granny Smith
   apples, peeled, cut into
   1/4-inch pieces
   (about 4 cups)
1 cup golden raisins
1 cup chopped seeded plum
   tomatoes
1 tablespoon chopped fresh
   mint
1 French bread baguette, cut
   into 1/3-inch-thick slices
Olive oil for brushing
Roasted Garlic (at left)
12 ounces fresh soft
   goat cheese (such as
   Montrachet), at room
   temperature

Cook the brown sugar and vinegar together in a large heavy saucepan over medium heat until the brown sugar dissolves, stirring constantly. Add the minced garlic, gingerroot, cayenne pepper and cinnamon stick and mix well. Simmer for 8 minutes or until the mixture reaches a syrup consistency and is reduced to 1/2 cup. Stir in the apples and raisins. Bring the mixture to a boil over high heat, stirring constantly. Boil for 10 minutes or until the apples are tender, stirring frequently. Cool to room temperature. Remove and discard the cinnamon stick. Stir in the tomatoes and mint. Arrange the bread slices on a baking sheet and brush with the olive oil. Bake at 450 degrees for 8 minutes or until golden brown and crisp. Spread each toast slice with Roasted Garlic. Top with the cheese and apple chutney. You may prepare the apple chutney 3 days ahead. Refrigerate, covered, until serving time.

*Yield: 6 to 8 servings*

# New England Clam Chowder

*Most people's favorite, whether in the North, South, East, or West, this was such a favorite at Johnston Street Cafe.*

2 dozen clams, scrubbed, or
   2 (7-ounce) cans clams
3 cups water
8 ounces sliced bacon, cut
   into 1-inch pieces
2 tablespoons butter
4 cups chopped onions
1/3 cup flour
6 potatoes, peeled, cut into
   1/2-inch pieces
   (about 7 cups)
1 1/2 teaspoons thyme
Ground pepper to taste
2 cups milk
2 cups heavy cream
1/4 cup chopped fresh
   Italian parsley

Combine the clams and water in a large pot. Cook, covered, over medium heat until the clams open. Remove from the heat. Cool slightly. Remove the clams from the shells and chop the clams. Strain and reserve the cooking liquid. Cook the bacon in the pot over low heat until brown, stirring frequently. Add the butter and onions. Sauté until the onions are tender. Stir in the flour and cook for 1 minute, stirring constantly. Add the clams, reserved cooking liquid, potatoes, thyme, pepper, milk and cream and mix well. Cook over medium heat until very hot, stirring constantly. Do not allow the mixture to boil or it will curdle. Taste and adjust the seasonings. Stir in the parsley.

*Yield: 12 servings*

# Courtland Chicken Stew

1 (4- to 5-pound) hen
8 large potatoes, peeled
2 large onions, finely
  chopped
4 (16-ounce) cans tomatoes
1 (12-ounce) can tomato
  paste
1 tablespoon salt
1/3 teaspoon black pepper
1/4 teaspoon red pepper
2 tablespoons vinegar
1 cup (2 sticks) butter,
  softened
2 (17-ounce) cans
  cream-style white corn

Boil the hen in just enough water to cover in a stockpot for 1 hour or until cooked through; cool. Chop the chicken, discarding the skin and bones. Return the chicken to the cooking liquid in the stockpot. Add the potatoes, onions, tomatoes, tomato paste, salt, black pepper, red pepper, vinegar and butter and mix well. Simmer, covered, over low heat for 3 to 4 hours or until the potatoes are cooked through. Remove and mash the potatoes. Return the potatoes to the stockpot. Add the corn and stir to mix. Cook for 1 hour longer or until of the desired consistency. Season with additional salt and pepper if necessary.

*Yield: 30 servings*

*Years ago when I co-edited* Cotton Country Cooking *with my good friend Katherine Wilks, Courtland Stew was included in the book, and I must include it here. I've often said that the best thing that came out of writing* Cotton Country *for me was creating such a wonderful friendship with such a great lady.*

# A Salad Medley

*This recipe was given to me by Scott Curry, a wonderful chef and friend.*
*He and his wife Meg bought Johnston Street Cafe from me.*
*It is now Curry's on Johnston Street.*

2 tablespoons butter
1/2 cup chopped walnuts
3 tablespoons brown sugar
Mixed salad greens such as
    romaine, green leaf
    lettuce and Boston lettuce
1 firm pear
3 scallions, chopped
3 to 4 ounces crumbled bleu
    cheese
Balsamic Vinaigrette (below)

Melt the butter in a heavy skillet over medium heat. Add the walnuts and brown sugar and sauté until the walnuts begin to soften. Remove from the skillet to cool. Rinse the salad greens; drain. Tear into bite-size pieces and place in a large bowl. Cut the pear into small pieces just before serving. Add the pear, walnut mixture, scallions, bleu cheese and Balsamic Vinaigrette to the salad greens and toss to mix. Serve immediately.

*Yield: 4 to 6 servings*

## Herbed Muffins

2 cups flour
1 tablespoon baking
    powder
1/2 teaspoon salt
2/3 cup shredded Swiss
    cheese
1 teaspoon chopped fresh
    dillweed
1 teaspoon chopped fresh
    thyme
2 eggs, well beaten
1 cup milk
1/2 cup (1 stick) butter,
    melted, slightly cooled

## Balsamic Vinaigrette

1 teaspoon dry mustard
1/2 teaspoon seasoned salt
1/4 teaspoon freshly ground
    pepper
3 tablespoons balsamic
    vinegar
2 tablespoons sugar
1/2 teaspoon onion juice
1 garlic clove, crushed
3/4 cup olive oil

Combine the dry mustard, seasoned salt and pepper in a bowl and mix well. Stir in the vinegar, sugar, onion juice and garlic. Let stand for 1 hour. Strain the mixture through a fine sieve to remove the garlic just before serving. Add the olive oil in a fine stream, whisking constantly until blended.

Sift the flour, baking powder and salt into a bowl. Add the cheese, dillweed and thyme and stir to mix. Combine the eggs, milk and butter in a bowl and mix well. Add to the dry ingredients and stir just until moistened. Spoon into 12 well greased muffin cups. Bake at 400 degrees for 20 minutes. Remove from the pan. Serve immediately.

*Yield 12 (3-inch) muffins*

# Chocolate Trifle with Black Cherries and Pears

*A shortcut would be to make the custard in the microwave.*

5¹/2 ounces bittersweet
   chocolate, chopped
6 egg yolks
2 cups sugar
1 teaspoon vanilla extract
¹/4 cup cornstarch
3 cups milk
2 packages (6 ounces or
   more) biscotti
¹/4 cup amaretto
2 (15-ounce) cans pitted
   black cherries, drained
2 (15-ounce) cans pear
   halves, drained, sliced
1 cup whipping cream,
   stiffly whipped

Melt the chocolate in the top of a double boiler set over simmering water, stirring frequently. Remove from the heat. Combine the egg yolks, sugar, vanilla and cornstarch in a bowl and mix until well blended. Heat the milk in a small saucepan until almost boiling. Pour over the egg yolk mixture, whisking vigorously. Pour the mixture into a medium saucepan. Cook over low heat for 6 to 8 minutes or until thickened, stirring constantly. Stir in the chocolate. Let stand until cool. Layer the biscotti, amaretto, chocolate custard, black cherries and pears ¹/2 at a time in a large serving dish or trifle bowl. Pipe the whipped cream over the top in a decorative fashion. Garnish with chocolate curls or shavings. You may substitute 5¹/2 ounces of semisweet chocolate chips for the bittersweet chocolate.

*Yield: 6 to 8 servings*

*This recipe was given to me by Gillian Spencer Pilgrim and is authentically English. Gillian is from England and is married to our sweet friend Trip Pilgrim, son of Liz and Harold.*

# Sweetheart Dinner

*Jalapeño Cheese Squares*
*Mixed Green Salad with Citrus Vinaigrette*
*Grilled Peppered Tenderloin with Wine Mushroom Sauce*
*Asparagus Dijon*
*Horseradish, Bacon and Chive Mashed Potatoes*
*Crème Brûlée • Wine*

Some of my very favorite people were at this cooking class. I actually did this menu twice for two different dinner clubs: Glen and Wally Terry's, and Elaine and Preston Maxey's dinner clubs. They were very enthusiastic. Everyone had a sweetheart. All the sauces may be done the day before and asparagus could be cooked, drained, patted dry, and refrigerated in layers with paper towels between. The Crème Brûlée could be done the day before and refrigerated with final sugar caramelizing just before serving. The tenderloin may be marinated and grilled early in the day. It should be served at room temperature. The Wine Mushroom Sauce can be prepared ahead of time and reheated. Potatoes need to be prepared an hour or two before guests arrive. You could cut potatoes up early in the day, cover with water and refrigerate to keep them from turning brown. We had some real fun at this class—I always let students caramelize their own sugar for their brûlée, with the blow torch, yes, a real "shop" blow torch. What a hoot! You may also buy the smaller version of a brûlée torch at Williams-Sonoma. My daughter Sheri Hofherr is a wonderful cook and she loves to serve this menu.

# Jalapeño Cheese Squares

4 cups (16 ounces) shredded
    Cheddar cheese
4 eggs, beaten
3 drained canned jalapeño
    chiles, seeded, chopped
1 (2-ounce) jar chopped
    pimento, drained
1 teaspoon minced onion

Combine the cheese, eggs, jalapeño chiles, pimento and onion in a bowl and mix well. Spread evenly in a lightly greased 8×8-inch baking pan. Bake at 350 degrees for 30 to 40 minutes or until brown and bubbly. Let stand for 10 minutes. Cut into squares and serve immediately.

*Yield: 3 dozen*

# Mixed Green Salad with Citrus Vinaigrette

2 heads Bibb lettuce
2 heads leaf lettuce
6 carrots, sliced
6 zucchini, sliced
6 yellow squash, sliced
10 plum tomatoes (Roma
    tomatoes), sliced
Citrus Vinaigrette (below)

Rinse the Bibb and leaf lettuce and pat or spin dry. Tear the lettuce into bite-size pieces and place in a large salad bowl. Add the carrots, zucchini, yellow squash and tomatoes. Pour Citrus Vinaigrette over the salad just before serving and toss to coat.

*Yield: 20 to 25 servings*

## Citrus Vinaigrette

2 cups canola oil
1/2 cup orange juice
1/2 cup lime juice
2 tablespoons minced fresh
    cilantro
2 tablespoons raspberry
    preserves
Salt and pepper to taste

Combine the canola oil, orange juice, lime juice, cilantro, raspberry preserves, salt and pepper in a food processor or 1-quart jar with a tight-fitting lid. Process or shake vigorously until well mixed.

*If you have large quantities of lettuce to wash for many guests, use a clean cotton pillow slip to store them in after they have been washed. The cotton pillow slip will absorb the moisture and you do not have to use a salad spinner. Refrigerate in the pillow slip.*

# Grilled Peppered Tenderloin with Wine Mushroom Sauce

1 (6- to 7-pound) fillet of
   beef
1 cup olive oil
1/2 cup red wine
Cracked pepper to taste
2 garlic cloves, minced
   (optional)
Wine Mushroom Sauce
   (below)

Place the beef in a shallow glass dish. Combine the olive oil, wine, cracked pepper and garlic in a small bowl and mix well. Pour over the beef, turning to coat. Marinate, covered, in the refrigerator for 1 hour, turning occasionally. Drain the beef, discarding the marinade. Rub with additional cracked pepper. Grill the beef on a gas grill on High for 5 minutes. Turn the beef. Grill for 5 minutes longer. Reduce the grill temperature to Medium. Grill for 20 minutes longer or until a meat thermometer inserted in the thickest portion registers 140 degrees for rare or 160 degrees for medium. Let stand for 10 minutes before slicing. Serve slices with warm Wine Mushroom Sauce or a simple horseradish sauce spooned over the top.

*Yield: 10 to 12 servings*

*This Grilled Peppered Tenderloin is Dr. Bill's recipe. He uses lots of cracked black pepper.*

## Wine Mushroom Sauce

1 1/2 teaspoons unsalted
   butter
1/2 cup sliced fresh wild
   mushrooms
1/2 teaspoon chopped fresh
   thyme
1/2 cup wine
1 1/4 cups veal stock or beef
   broth
1 teaspoon lemon juice
1/4 teaspoon salt
2 tablespoons cornstarch
2 tablespoons water

Melt the butter in a heavy medium saucepan over medium-high heat. Sauté the mushrooms and thyme in the butter for 3 minutes or until tender. Add the wine, stock, lemon juice and salt and mix well. Bring to a boil, stirring constantly. Whisk the cornstarch and water together in a small cup. Add to the sauce. Return the mixture to a boil. Boil until thickened, stirring constantly.

## Asparagus Dijon

1¹/2 pounds fresh
  asparagus spears,
  trimmed
¹/4 cup whipping cream,
  whipped
2 tablespoons mayonnaise
1 scallion, chopped
1 tablespoon Dijon
  mustard

Cook the asparagus in
boiling water to cover
in a saucepan for 4 to
6 minutes or until tender-
crisp; drain. Rinse under
cold running water to stop
the cooking process and
retain the bright green
color of the asparagus.
Arrange the asparagus on
a serving platter. Combine
the whipped cream, mayon-
naise, scallion and Dijon
mustard in a bowl and mix
well. Spoon the sauce over
the asparagus and serve.

*Yield: 4 to 6 servings*

# Horseradish, Bacon and Chive Mashed Potatoes

*This recipe was given to me by Scott Curry, a great chef trained in Atlanta in the finer restaurants. He now owns my former restaurant, Johnston Street Cafe.*

4 baking potatoes, peeled,
  chopped, cooked
¹/2 cup chopped crisp-cooked
  bacon
¹/2 cup chopped fresh chives
¹/4 cup prepared horseradish
¹/4 cup (¹/2 stick) butter,
  softened
¹/2 cup heavy cream
Salt and pepper to taste

Place the potatoes in a mixing bowl and beat until fluffy. Add the bacon, chives, horseradish, butter, cream, salt and pepper and beat lightly until of the desired consistency.

*Yield: 4 to 6 servings*

# Chocolate Hearts

4 ounces sweetened
  chocolate, coarsely
  chopped
Melted white chocolate

Place the sweetened chocolate in the top of a double boiler set over simmering water. Temper the chocolate, stirring constantly with a rubber spatula for 15 to 20 minutes or until the chocolate is completely melted and smooth. Do not rush the tempering process and do not let the simmering water come to a boil at any time. Remove from the heat. Pour the chocolate onto a parchment or waxed paper-lined baking sheet. Spread the chocolate evenly to ¹/16 to ¹/8 inch thick. Let stand until the chocolate loses its sheen and is almost dry but not completely hardened. Press a small heart-shaped cookie cutter firmly into the chocolate. Repeat, pressing as many heart shapes as possible. Allow the chocolate to set or harden. Slide each heart carefully off the parchment paper using a metal spatula. Drizzle the chocolate hearts with melted white chocolate.

*Yield: (about) 6 chocolate hearts*

# Crème Brûlée

3 cups heavy cream
6 tablespoons sugar
6 egg yolks
2 teaspoons vanilla extract
1/2 cup granulated white
    sugar or light brown sugar

Heat the cream in the top of a double boiler over boiling water. Stir in 6 tablespoons sugar. Beat the egg yolks in a small bowl until light. Pour over the hot cream mixture gradually, stirring vigorously. Remove from the heat. Stir in the vanilla. Strain the mixture through a fine sieve into a baking pan. Place the pan in a larger pan. Fill the larger pan with 1 inch of hot water. Bake at 300 degrees for 35 minutes or until a silver knife inserted in the center comes out clean; do not overbake. Remove from the oven; the custard will continue to cook from its retained heat. Cool slightly. Chill thoroughly, covered, in the refrigerator. Sprinkle the surface of the chilled custard with 1 tablespoon sugar. Set the pan on a bed of cracked ice in a larger pan. Broil until the sugar is melted and brown. Garnish with Chocolate Hearts (page 102). Serve immediately or chill and serve cold.

*Yield: 6 to 8 servings*

*I always use the blow torch to caramelize the sugar— much faster and your custard remains cool.*

*When using a blow torch, start on the outside of the dish and work your way towards the center.*

# The French Connection—A Dinner in Provence

*Crostini (page 94)* • *Tapenade Olive Spread*
*Fresh Mozzarella Tomato Basil Salad*
*Rack of Lamb* • *Potato Gratin with Sorrel Cream*
*Stuffed Zucchini* • *Divine Flourless Chocolate Cake*

One of the most wonderful experiences of my life was the delightful trip to France where I enjoyed "Cooking with Friends," directed by Kathy Alex, with my sweet friend, Jackie Guice, and my daughter, Libby Sims Patrick. Kathy Alex has bought Julia Child's chateau in southern France, near Grasse and conducts a cooking school there. We had "hands-on" training, the French way, tours of three-star restaurants, and visits to the fabulous open-air markets and a cheese cave (where they age their finer cheeses). We learned so much about the French in general, and we were fascinated by the different varieties of vegetables that they grow. Following the cooking classes, we traveled to Vence, France, to visit Nall, the most talented artist, and his beautiful wife, Tuscia, for a gala on the grounds of their estate, honoring Alabama artists. This menu may be easily prepared as the tomatoes and fresh mozzarella may be sliced at the last minute. The pesto for the lamb may be made several days ahead and refrigerated, as can the tapenade. The potatoes can be simmered for the four minutes, removed to a buttered baking dish with the milk mixture poured over and refrigerated. On the afternoon of your dinner, remove the dish from the refrigerator an hour and a half before you bake and serve. The Stuffed Zucchini may be prepared early in the day except for baking. The Divine Chocolate Cake does beautifully made the day before and refrigerated. You perhaps will want to set up a buffet in the dining room or serve the plates from the kitchen if you have a small group. I just love a simple bouquet of tulips in a crystal bowl (1 color) for a centerpiece and of course white or cream candles in silver candlesticks. Dim the lights and Bon Appétit! Oops, I forgot to discuss the lamb preparation. It takes a very short time and can be done as your guests are entertained by your husband. Have him pass the tapenade with crostini while you are doing last minute lamb preparation. Prepare your pesto for the lamb the day before.

# Fresh Mozzarella Tomato Basil Salad

8 ounces fresh mozzarella
  cheese, drained
2 large red tomatoes, sliced
2 large yellow tomatoes,
  sliced
1 cup pear tomatoes, cut
  into halves
1/2 teaspoon salt
2 tablespoons extra-virgin
  olive oil
Freshly ground pepper
1/2 cup thinly sliced or
  chopped fresh basil

Slice the cheese into 1/4-inch slices. Layer the tomato slices and cheese slices alternately on a serving platter. Scatter the pear tomato halves over the top. Sprinkle with the salt and drizzle with the olive oil. Chill, covered, for 4 hours. Sprinkle with pepper and basil just before serving. Garnish with a sprig of basil.

*Yield: 6 to 8 servings*

# Rack of Lamb

*Be sure your butcher trims between the bones.*
*This is called "Frenching" the lamb.*

1 1/2 cups packed fresh
  parsley (leaves and stems)
6 tablespoons chopped fresh
  rosemary
6 tablespoons grated
  Parmesan cheese
3 garlic cloves
9 tablespoons olive oil
Salt and pepper to taste
1 (4 1/2- to 5-pound) rack
  of lamb, at room
  temperature

Combine the parsley, rosemary, cheese and garlic in a food processor and process until of a coarse paste consistency. Add the olive oil in a fine stream, processing constantly. Season the pesto with salt and pepper. Place the lamb on a rimmed baking sheet. Sprinkle with salt and pepper. Spread the pesto evenly over the rounded side of the lamb, using all of the pesto. Roast on the center oven rack at 450 degrees for 10 minutes. Reduce the oven temperature to 400 degrees. Roast for 15 minutes longer for medium-rare, or to the desired degree of doneness. Cut the lamb, between the bones, into chops. Divide the chops among 6 dinner plates. Garnish with fresh rosemary sprigs.

*Yield: 6 servings*

# Tapenade Olive Spread

1 pound niçoise olives,
  pitted
2 anchovy fillets
1 garlic clove, chopped
2 tablespoons drained
  capers
Freshly ground pepper
  to taste
3 tablespoons olive oil

Combine the olives, anchovies, garlic, capers and pepper in a food processor and process until puréed. Add the olive oil in a fine stream, processing constantly. Spread over small toasts or Crostini (page 110) and serve.

*Yield: (about) 2 cups*

# *Potato Gratin with Sorrel Cream*

2 pounds boiling potatoes,
   peeled
2 cups heavy cream
1 cup (or more) milk
Freshly grated nutmeg
2 teaspoons salt
Freshly ground pepper
1/2 cup heavy cream
1 bunch sorrel, stemmed,
   thinly sliced, or 1 cup
   thinly sliced watercress

*Sorrel is a hearty herb belonging to the buckwheat family and has some degree of acidity. Its prime season is spring, and it is used in meats, vegetables, soups, and omelets. It is high in vitamin A.*

Cut the potatoes into 1/8-inch-thick slices and place in a large saucepan. Add 2 cups heavy cream, the milk, nutmeg, salt and pepper and mix well. Bring to a simmer. Cook for 4 minutes. Remove the potatoes with a slotted spoon and arrange in a single layer in a buttered 12-inch oval gratin dish. Taste the milk mixture and adjust the seasonings if necessary. Pour over the potatoes, adding additional milk if needed to keep the potatoes well covered with liquid during baking. Bake at 375 degrees for 20 minutes or just until the potatoes are tender. Remove from the oven. Increase the oven temperature to 450 degrees. Combine 1/2 cup heavy cream and the sorrel in a small saucepan. Heat over low heat until the sorrel has melted and become creamy, stirring constantly. Pour the sorrel cream over the cooked potatoes. Bake at 450 degrees for 8 to 10 minutes or until the surface is light brown, or broil briefly until light brown. You may keep the dish warm in the oven (turned off) for 30 to 40 minutes until serving time. May be prepared 1 or 2 hours in advance and reheated in a moderate oven for 10 to 15 minutes or until the gratin begins to bubble.

*Yield: 6 to 8 servings*

# Stuffed Zucchini

*They have the most precious small, round zucchini in France. These were so attractive stuffed. They had the same taste as our slender zucchini. Persillade is a combination of parsley and garlic*

2 tablespoons chopped
   Italian flat-leaf parsley
1 garlic clove, chopped
8 small zucchini (about
   5 ounces), unpeeled,
   rinsed, stems removed
4 to 6 tablespoons olive oil
1 onion, finely chopped
Salt to taste
8 ounces bulk pork sausage,
   cooked, drained
Pepper to taste
Pinch of herbes de Provence
1 cup fresh bread crumbs
1/4 cup freshly grated
   Parmesan cheese
1 or 2 eggs
Dry bread crumbs

Combine the parsley and garlic in a small bowl and mix well to make a persillade. Cut each zucchini in half lengthwise. Remove the flesh with a melon baller and reserve, leaving shells. Bring enough water to cover the zucchini shells to a boil in a stockpot. Add the zucchini shells. Parboil for 6 to 7 minutes or until the shells are slightly softened. Remove carefully with a slotted spoon. Drain, cut side down, on paper towels. Chop the reserved zucchini flesh. Heat 2 tablespoons of the olive oil in a skillet over low heat. Add the onion. Cook for 10 minutes or until tender but not brown. Add the zucchini flesh and season with salt. Cook for 15 minutes or until very tender and reduced in volume, but not brown, stirring and tossing constantly. Remove to a bowl. Add the sausage, pepper, herbes de Provence, persillade, fresh bread crumbs and cheese and mix well. Add 1 egg and 1 or 2 tablespoons of the remaining olive oil and mix with your hands, adding 1 egg if the stuffing is too dry. Arrange the zucchini shells not touching in a shallow baking dish. Sprinkle the shells with salt and drizzle with 1/2 of the remaining olive oil. Divide the stuffing among the shells. Press in place. Sprinkle with the bread crumbs. Drizzle with the remaining olive oil. Pour enough water into the dish to measure 1/2 inch. Bake at 350 degrees for 30 to 45 minutes. Serve hot, warm or at room temperature.

*Yield: 8 servings*

*Simone Beck, lovingly known as Simka, shared this recipe. Julia Child and Simone Beck wrote* Mastering the Art of French Cooking *while living in châteaus side by side at La Pitchoune where we were privileged to stay. Simone has now passed away and Julia no longer lives in France.*

# Divine Flourless Chocolate Cake

8 ounces dark bittersweet
  chocolate, chopped
3¹/2 tablespoons water
1¹/2 tablespoons instant
  coffee crystals
1 cup (2 sticks) unsalted
  butter, cut into small
  pieces
4 jumbo eggs
1 cup sugar
¹/2 teaspoon vanilla extract
Chocolate Glaze (at left)

Butter a 10-inch cake pan generously. Line the bottom of the pan with buttered parchment paper. Refrigerate until time to fill. Combine the chopped chocolate, water and coffee crystals in the top of a double boiler set over simmering water. Heat until the chocolate is almost completely melted. Remove from the heat. Stir until smooth. Add the butter and stir vigorously until the butter is melted. Remove the top of the double boiler and set aside to cool. Beat the eggs and sugar in a mixing bowl until the mixture is pale and forms a ribbon when the beaters are lifted from the batter. Add the vanilla and cooled chocolate mixture and mix well. Pour into the prepared pan and rap the bottom of the pan sharply against the counter once to break any air bubbles. Bake at 350 degrees for 40 to 55 minutes or until the cake tests done, rotating the pan occasionally to ensure even baking. You may test for doneness by inserting a wooden pick in the center of the cake after 40 minutes of the baking time. The tester should come out moist, showing a creamy consistency in the center. Cool on a wire rack. Invert onto a serving plate. Spread Chocolate Glaze over the cooled cake and serve.

*Yield: 8 to 10 servings*

## Chocolate Glaze

2 cups (12 ounces)
  semisweet chocolate
  chips
1 cup heavy cream

Microwave the chocolate chips in a microwave-safe container on Medium until melted. Add the cream and stir until smooth.

# A Birthday Dinner

*Crostini with Tomato Goat Cheese Spread*
*Artichoke and Oyster Soup*
*San Francisco Salad • Roasted Tuscan Pork*
*Soft Polenta with Swiss and Parmesan Cheese*
*Beef Brisket with Gravy • Dill Drop Scones*
*Bill Sims Jr. Fudge Pie with Famous Chocolate Fudge Sauce or*
*Birthday Dinner Cake with Snow White Frosting*

Birthdays are so special and it's always fun to gather friends, family, and balloons for the celebration. Birthdays in our family have always been special and even though the grown children live in other cities, I always call early morning on their birthdays with a squawky rendition of "Happy Birthday" from Mom and Doc. We try to be together on birthdays as much as possible. This menu is a favorite of mine. The Crostini, Tomato Goat Cheese Spread, soup, and cake or fudge pie can be done a day ahead, or the Crostini can be done much ahead and frozen. The roasted pork and the polenta may be prepared early afternoon of your birthday party. If you choose the Beef Brisket, it can be cooked the day before and reheated. Your salad greens can be washed the day before and stored in a sealable plastic bag or a clean cotton pillow slip in the refrigerator. The dressing may be made a few days ahead and the salad tossed just before serving. Of course, I really like a buffet method of serving unless you're having a small family party. Decorate with balloons, banners, placecards, and flowers in a crystal vase. My favorites are tulips or lilies. So easy. If you have no flowers you can always use magnolia leaves laid on the table with votives nestled in. The pork dish in this menu is done by my friend John Wilks, and is a Mauby's favorite.

# Crostini with
# Tomato Goat Cheese Spread

*Crostini means "little crusts" in Italian and originated as a clever way
to use the last bit of bread from yesterday's loaf. These are small toasts made
by brushing small baguette slices with good olive oil and toasting them in
the oven. They are topped with a variety of mixtures from simple to complex.
These usually precede a meal in Italy.*

*Olive oil can be confusing.
Virgin olive oil means
that the oil is extracted
from handpicked olives
that are cold pressed
without the use of heat or
chemicals. Cold pressed,
the lesser quality, is
from subsequent pressings
and is extracted using
heat. These are simple
olive oils and are not as
fruity or flavorful.*

3 French baguettes
1/2 cup extra-virgin olive oil
1/2 cup finely chopped fresh
    dillweed
Chopped fresh thyme and
    rosemary
Minced garlic
Tomato Goat Cheese Spread
    (below)

Slice each baguette diagonally into 1/4-inch-thick slices. Arrange in a single layer on a parchment paper-lined baking sheet. Combine the olive oil, dillweed, thyme, rosemary and garlic in a bowl and mix well. Brush the tops of the baguette slices with the mixture. Bake at 300 degrees for 30 minutes or until crisp but not brown. May be prepared ahead. Top with Tomato Goat Cheese Spread.

*Yield: 12 servings*

## Tomato Goat Cheese Spread

2 (8-ounce) logs plain goat
    cheese, at room
    temperature
1/2 cup drained oil-pack
    sun-dried tomatoes,
    minced
8 fresh basil leaves, chopped
2 garlic cloves, minced
1/4 cup chopped pine nuts

Mash the goat cheese with a fork in a medium bowl. Add the tomatoes, basil, garlic and pine nuts and mix well. Pack into a serving bowl or crock. Chill, covered, for up to 4 days. Bring to room temperature before serving.

# Artichoke and Oyster Soup

1 cup (2 sticks) butter
1¹/4 cups flour
¹/2 cup chopped scallions
¹/4 cup chopped fresh parsley
1¹/2 teaspoons thyme
³/4 teaspoon cayenne pepper
3 cups chicken stock
8 cups heavy cream
2 pints oysters
2 (15-ounce) cans artichoke
   hearts, drained, chopped
Salt and black pepper
   to taste

Melt the butter in a skillet over medium heat. Add the flour and cook to make a roux, stirring constantly until smooth. Add the scallions, parsley, thyme and cayenne pepper and mix well; set aside. Bring the stock to a boil in a stockpot. Add the roux and stir until smooth. Add the cream, 2 cups at a time, stirring until smooth after each addition. Reduce the heat to a simmer. Add the undrained oysters and artichokes and mix well. Simmer until the soup is heated through and the oysters appear firm and done, stirring frequently to prevent scorching; do not boil. Season with salt and black pepper. Serve warm, garnished with chopped scallions or chives.

*Yield: 8 to 10 servings*

# San Francisco Salad

2 teaspoons sugar
4 garlic cloves
1 teaspoon oregano
¹/2 cup chopped red onion
¹/4 teaspoon salt
¹/4 teaspoon pepper
¹/2 cup red wine vinegar
1 cup chopped fresh parsley
¹/2 cup vegetable oil
1 cup chopped walnuts
3 tablespoons butter
¹/2 cup sugar
1 tablespoon coarsely
   ground pepper
8 ounces mixed salad greens
Spinach leaves
³/4 cup dried cranberries
8 ounces feta cheese

Combine 2 teaspoons sugar, the garlic, oregano, red onion, salt, ¹/4 teaspoon pepper, vinegar and parsley in a food processor or blender and process until well mixed. Add the oil in a fine stream, processing constantly. Chill, covered, until ready to serve. Sauté the walnuts in the butter in a skillet for 5 minutes. Combine ¹/2 cup sugar and 1 tablespoon pepper in a bowl and mix well. Add the walnuts and mix well. Combine the walnut mixture, mixed salad greens, spinach, cranberries and cheese in a large salad bowl and toss to mix. Pour the dressing over the salad and toss to mix.

*Yield: 6 to 8 servings*

*This soup is a favorite at Mauby's Restaurant in Birmingham. San Francisco Salad comes from Karen Love, Katherine Wilks' daughter, who lives in Birmingham and entertains a lot. Karen is John Wilks' sister.*

# Roasted Tuscan Pork

Four roasted garlic bulbs
2¹/₂ pounds boneless pork
  loin, trimmed
¹/₄ cup each chopped fresh
  rosemary, basil, oregano,
  parsley and thyme
Garlic-infused olive oil
  (reserved from roasting
  garlic)

Squeeze the roasted garlic from each clove and spread over the pork loin to coat. Mix the chopped herbs on waxed paper. Roll the pork loin in the herbs to coat. Place in a roasting pan. Roast at 375 degrees until cooked through or until a meat thermometer inserted in the thickest portion reads medium-well. Let stand for 5 minutes before slicing. Slice and drizzle with garlic-infused olive oil. Serve over Soft Polenta (below). To roast the garlic, slice the tops off 4 garlic bulbs. Stand the bulbs cut side up in a small baking dish and drizzle with olive oil. Roast until the garlic is soft and creamy and is easily squeezed from each clove.

*Yield: 6 servings*

*John and Mary Wilks own and operate Mauby's Restaurant, one of the most famous in Birmingham. Mauby's has won many awards and continues to be a very popular place. John credits the fine meals to Chef Johnny Showers and Sous Chef Richard Showers, hardworking brothers.*

# Soft Polenta

3 cups vegetable or chicken
  stock
3/4 cup finely ground yellow
  cornmeal
1/3 cup sour cream
4 ounces Swiss cheese,
  shredded
3 ounces grated Parmesan
  cheese
Sea salt and freshly ground
  pepper to taste

Bring the stock to a boil in a large saucepan. Add the cornmeal gradually, whisking constantly to prevent lumping. Reduce the heat to low. Cook for 30 to 45 minutes, stirring occasionally with a wooden spoon to prevent scorching. Stir in the sour cream, Swiss cheese and Parmesan cheese. Season with sea salt and pepper. Keep warm over low heat. Stir in additional stock, if necessary, to maintain a soft consistency.

*Yield: 6 to 8 servings*

# Beef Brisket with Gravy

*My sweet friend, Peggy Burkhart from Lexington, Kentucky, shared this recipe
with me. Our friendship dates back to medical school. Peg is a great cook.*

1 (3-pound) beef brisket,
   untrimmed
Salt and pepper to taste
Paprika
4 large garlic cloves, sliced
1 large onion, sliced
1/2 to 1 cup water
1/2 cup flour
1 1/2 cups water

Arrange the brisket in a baking pan. Sprinkle
with salt and pepper. Season generously with
paprika. Arrange the garlic and onion over the
top. Sprinkle with additional paprika. Bake,
uncovered, at 325 degrees for 45 minutes or
until brown. Add 1/2 to 1 cup water and cover
the pan tightly with foil. Bake for 3 hours
longer or until the brisket is fork-tender,
basting every 30 minutes with the pan
drippings. Remove the brisket to a warm
platter. Make gravy by whisking the flour and
1 1/2 cups water into the pan drippings. Stir
until smooth. Serve with mashed potatoes and
fresh green beans.

*Yield: 6 to 8 servings*

# Dill Drop Scones

2 cups flour
2 1/2 teaspoons baking
   powder
1/4 teaspoon salt
2 tablespoons butter, cut
   into pieces
2 teaspoons chopped chives
   or scallions
2 teaspoons chopped fresh
   dillweed
Freshly ground pepper
1/4 cup small curd cottage
   cheese
2/3 cup milk

Sift the flour, baking powder and salt into a
large bowl. Cut or rub in the butter using a
pastry blender or your fingertips until the
mixture resembles coarse crumbs. Stir in the
chives, dillweed and pepper until well mixed.
Make a well in the center of the mixture. Pour
the cottage cheese and milk into the well and
stir with a fork just until combined. Drop by
tablespoonfuls 1 inch apart onto a large baking
sheet lined with greased parchment paper or
foil. Bake at 425 degrees for 15 minutes or
until risen and golden brown. Cool on the pan
for 2 minutes. Remove to a wire rack to cool
completely.

*Yield: 1 dozen scones*

# Bill Sims, Jr. Fudge Pie

*This is so quick and delicious. Add almond flavoring or amaretto to the fudge sauce if desired. The sauce makes a wonderful filling for tart shells and also works great as a fondue.*

1/2 cup (1 stick) butter, melted
1 cup sugar
1/2 cup flour
3 tablespoons baking cocoa
2 eggs, lightly beaten
1 teaspoon vanilla extract
Famous Chocolate Fudge Sauce (below)

Combine the butter, sugar, flour, baking cocoa, eggs and vanilla in a large bowl and mix well. Pour into a greased 9-inch pie plate. Bake at 350 degrees for 25 minutes. Serve with ice cream and warm Famous Chocolate Fudge Sauce.

*Yield: 6 to 8 servings*

## Dessert Coffees

*To make your own hot coffee drinks, start with 1/2 cup of hot, strong coffee and choose from the suggestions below and at right. Top off your steaming cup with some whipped cream and a large dash of cinnamon or nutmeg.*

*Café Alexander: Stir in 1 tablespoon crème de cacao and 1 tablespoon brandy.*

*Café Benedictine: Stir in 2 tablespoons Benedictine and 2 tablespoons light cream.*

*Café Caribe: Stir in 1 tablespoon coffee liqueur and 1 tablespoon rum.*

# Famous Chocolate Fudge Sauce

7 ounces unsweetened chocolate
1 3/4 cups sugar
1 tablespoon butter
1/4 teaspoon salt
1 (12-ounce) can evaporated milk
1 teaspoon vanilla extract

Melt the chocolate in the top of a double boiler set over hot water. Add the sugar, butter and salt, stirring until the mixture is smooth. Add the evaporated milk. Cook until thickened, stirring frequently. Remove from the heat. Stir in the vanilla. May cook in the microwave in a large glass bowl on High for 3 1/2 to 4 minutes, stirring 3 to 4 times during cooking.

# Birthday Dinner Cake with Snow White Frosting

2 cups flour
2 teaspoons baking powder
1/4 teaspoon salt
4 eggs
2 cups sugar
1 cup milk
1/2 cup (1 stick) butter
Lemon Curd Filling (page 144)
Snow White Frosting (below)

Sift the flour, baking powder and salt together. Beat the eggs in a bowl until thick and pale yellow. Add the sugar gradually, beating until blended. Add the sifted dry ingredients gradually, mixing well after each addition. Combine the milk and butter in a saucepan and heat just to the boiling point, stirring until the butter is melted. Add to the egg mixture and mix quickly. Pour into 2 well greased and floured 9-inch cake pans. Bake at 350 degrees for 20 to 25 minutes or until the cake tests done. Cool on a wire rack. Spread Lemon Curd Filling between the layers. Spread Snow White Frosting over the top and side of the cake.

*Yield: 12 servings*

## Snow White Frosting

2 egg whites
1 1/2 cups sugar
1/4 teaspoon salt
1/3 cup water
2 teaspoons light corn syrup
1 teaspoon vanilla extract

Combine the egg whites, sugar, salt, water and corn syrup in the top of a double boiler and whisk for 1 minute or until thoroughly mixed. Heat over boiling water, beating at high speed for 6 to 8 minutes or until stiff peaks form. Remove from the heat. Add the vanilla and beat until thick and of the desired spreading consistency.

## Dessert Coffees

*Café Colombian: Stir in 2 tablespoons coffee liqueur and 1 tablespoon coffee-flavored syrup.*

*Café Israel: Stir in 2 tablespoons chocolate-flavored syrup and 2 tablespoons orange liqueur.*

*Café Nut: Stir in 2 tablespoons chocolate-mint liqueur.*

*Irish Coffee: Stir in 1 tablespoon Irish whiskey and 2 teaspoons sugar.*

*Orange-Brandy Coffee: Stir in 1 tablespoon orange liqueur and 1 tablespoon brandy. If desired, sprinkle finely shredded orange peel atop whipped cream instead of cinnamon or nutmeg.*

# A Traditional Holiday Dinner with a Twist

*Crostini • Red Onion Marmalade*
*Shrimp Paste*
*Congealed Waldorf Salad*
*Roasted Turkey with Thyme and Rosemary*
*Corn Bread Dressing*
*Sweet Potato Casserole*
*Roasted Whole Pumpkin with*
*Wild Mushroom Bread Pudding*
*Cranberry Chutney • Green Things*
*Pumpkin Pie with Caramel Pecan Sauce*

The holidays are about traditions. They are a time to have your loved ones over to a house brimming with good smells and good thoughts. We have so much to be thankful for, and in light of the last year's occurrences, we are even more thankful for our families and our country, where we are free. Bonnie Bailey, the inspiration for my Johnston Street Cafe, has taught this class with me for many years. Joyce Nabors, a great cook and friend who helped me out with catering at Johnston Street Cafe, assisted us with this class. Most of these items on the menu can be prepared ahead except for the Turkey and Green Things. I always make the Cranberry Chutney days ahead along with the Crostini and Red Onion Marmalade. I prepare the Shrimp Paste, congealed salad, dressing, sweet potatoes, pumpkin with mushroom bread pudding and the pie on the day before and refrigerate of course. The "day of" remove all these items from the refrigerator and bake.

# Crostini with Red Onion Marmalade or Shrimp Paste

1/2 cup (1 stick) unsalted
  butter, melted
1/2 cup olive oil
1/2 teaspoon minced garlic
1 tablespoon mixed chopped
  fresh dillweed, chives,
  thyme and rosemary
1 to 3 French baguettes,
  sliced 1/4-inch thick
Red Onion Marmalade
  (below)
Shrimp Paste (at right)

Combine the butter, olive oil, garlic and herbs in a bowl and mix well. Brush each side of the baguette slices with the mixture. Arrange on a foil or parchment paper-lined baking sheet. Bake at 230 degrees for 45 minutes or until crispy. Cool on a wire rack. Serve with Red Onion Marmalade, Shrimp Paste or any savory topping desired.

*Misprint: Bake a 250°*

**Yield: variable**

*I used whole wheat baguettes*
*" " fresh chives & rosemary*
*and dried dill & thyme*

## Shrimp Paste

4 cups (16 ounces)
  shredded sharp
  Cheddar cheese
2 (4-ounce) cans small
  shrimp, drained
1 1/2 cups mayonnaise
2 tablespoons grated
  onion

Combine the cheese, shrimp, mayonnaise and onion in a large bowl and mix well with a fork. Chill, covered, for 4 hours or longer before serving.

## Red Onion Marmalade

2 large red onions, thinly
  sliced
3 tablespoons brown sugar
3/4 cup dry red wine
3 tablespoons balsamic
  vinegar
Salt and pepper to taste

*add: 1 tsp. minced garlic*

Combine the onions and brown sugar in a saucepan. Cook over medium heat for 20 to 30 minutes or until the onions begin to caramelize and turn golden brown, stirring frequently. Stir in the wine and vinegar. Bring to a boil over medium-high heat; reduce the heat. Cook over low heat for 15 minutes or until most of the liquid has been absorbed, stirring frequently. Season with salt and pepper. Chill, covered, for up to 3 weeks. Bring to room temperature before serving.

*Use Goatcheese instead of shrimp paste —
what we had at luncheon
I used whipped [?]*

## Extra Instructions for Roasting

### Choosing the turkey

*Look for a fresh unbasted turkey. A prebasted turkey is usually injected with a mixture of broth, vegetable oil, and seasonings; reading the label will help you tell if the turkey has been prebasted. If your local grocery store does not offer fresh unbasted turkeys, try to find a frozen one that hasn't been prebasted.*

### Thawing the turkey

*Leave the frozen turkey in its original packaging, and use one of the following thawing methods.*

*Place turkey in packaging in a large shallow pan in refrigerator for 3 to 4 days until thawed. Allow about 5 hours per pound.*

# Congealed Waldorf Salad

*This salad has always been John Caddell's favorite.*

1/2 envelope unflavored gelatin
1/4 cup cold water
1 (8-ounce) can juice-pack crushed pineapple
2 eggs, beaten
1/2 cup sugar
1/8 teaspoon salt
1/4 cup lemon juice
2 unpeeled apples, cored, finely chopped
1/2 cup finely chopped celery
1/2 cup broken pecans or walnuts
1/2 cup whipping cream, whipped

Soften the gelatin in the cold water in a small bowl and mix well. Drain the pineapple, reserving 1/2 cup of the liquid. Reserve 1/2 cup of the pineapple. Combine the reserved pineapple juice, eggs, sugar, salt and lemon juice in the top of a double boiler and mix well. Cook over hot water until thickened, stirring constantly. Stir in the gelatin mixture. Remove from the heat. Let stand until cool. Stir in the apples, celery, reserved pineapple and pecans. Fold in the whipped cream. Spoon into a lightly greased 5-cup mold or divide evenly among 10 custard cups sprayed with nonstick cooking spray. Chill until set.

*Yield: 10 servings*

# Turkey Broth for Dressing and Gravy

Turkey neck and gizzard
2 tablespoons vegetable oil
1 onion, cut into large chunks
1 carrot, cut into large chunks
2 to 3 ribs celery, cut into large chunks
8 cups water
2 teaspoons thyme, or several sprigs of fresh thyme
Salt and freshly ground pepper to taste

Brown the turkey neck and gizzard lightly in the oil in a heavy pot. Add the onion, carrot and celery. Cook until the vegetables are brown, stirring gently. Add the water, scraping the browned bits from the bottom of the pan. Cook for 10 minutes, stirring frequently. May add white wine, vermouth or additional water at this point. Cook, covered, for 2 hours for every 4 cups of broth, stirring occasionally. Add the thyme, salt and pepper. Strain the mixture. May be prepared 1 day ahead. Chill, covered, before straining.

# Roasted Turkey
# with Thyme and Rosemary

*My talented friend Bonnie Bailey and I have taught this class together
many times going back as far as the 1980s.*

1 (12-pound) fresh or frozen
 turkey, thawed
2 teaspoons dried thyme, or
 several sprigs of fresh
 thyme
3 sprigs of fresh rosemary
1 cup flour
Turkey Broth (page 118)

Arrange the turkey in a roasting pan. Sprinkle
with the thyme and rosemary. Insert sprigs of
thyme and rosemary into the cavity and under
the breast skin. Cover the breast with folded
foil. Roast at 325 degrees for 20 minutes
per pound, removing the foil 30 minutes
before the turkey is done. Let stand at room
temperature for 20 minutes. Remove to a
carving board. Discard the pan drippings,
reserving 1 cup. Sprinkle the flour over the
reserved drippings in the pan and mix well,
scraping the browned bits from the bottom of
the pan. Place the pan over two burners and
cook for 5 minutes or until the flour is cooked
and brown, stirring constantly. Add the desired
amount of Turkey Broth, whisking to dissolve
any lumps. Stir in additional water, if needed,
to make of a gravy consistency. Serve the
turkey with the gravy.

*Yield: 12 to 15 servings*

## Extra Instructions
## for Roasting

*Place turkey in packaging
in the sink and cover with
cold water; change water
frequently. Allow 30
minutes per pound.*

### Roasting the turkey

*When selecting a turkey,
buy a fresh one if possible.
Allow about 1 pound of
uncooked bird per person—
more if you want leftovers.*

*Make turkey stock with the
neck and giblets.*

*Remove the turkey from
the refrigerator 1 to
2 hours before roasting.*

*Preheat the oven to
425 degrees. Rinse the
turkey inside and out with
cold water. Dry with paper
towels. Lightly season the
turkey, inside and out, with
salt and pepper.*

## Extra Instructions for Roasting

*Place the turkey, breast side up, on a greased rack in a shallow roasting pan just large enough to hold it.*

*Put the turkey in the oven and immediately reduce the heat to 325 degrees. Roast the bird for about 20 minutes per pound for a stuffed bird and 16 minutes per pound for an unstuffed one.*

*The USDA specifies that cooking poultry to an internal temperature of 180 degrees will kill all bacteria that can cause illness.*

*Transfer the turkey to a carving board, cover loosely with foil and let rest for at least 15 minutes and up to 30 minutes before carving.*

*I never stuff my turkeys. The dressing or stuffing is a side dish*

# Corn Bread Dressing

4 onions, chopped
2 cups chopped celery
1/2 cup (1 stick) butter
10 cups crumbled corn bread
8 cups (about) strained
    Turkey Broth (page 118)
4 eggs, beaten
5 to 6 slices white bread,
    torn into small pieces
    (2 cups)

Sauté the onions and celery in the butter in a skillet until tender. Soften the corn bread crumbs in the Turkey Broth in a large bowl, using the desired amount of broth to make a moist but not soupy dressing. Add the onion mixture, eggs and white bread and mix well. Spoon into a greased 3-quart baking dish. Bake at 350 degrees for 40 minutes. You may use canned broth.

*Yield: 12 to 15 servings*

# Sweet Potato Casserole

1 cup chopped pecans
Melted butter
8 sweet potatoes, stewed
1 cup (2 sticks) butter or
    margarine, softened
2 1/4 cups sugar
1 cup milk
6 eggs, lightly beaten
1/3 cup frozen orange juice
    concentrate, thawed
Grated zest of 1 orange
1 teaspoon vanilla extract
1 teaspoon cinnamon
1/2 teaspoon nutmeg
1/2 teaspoon ground cloves

Combine the pecans and a small amount of melted butter in a small bowl and mix well. Peel and mash the potatoes while hot with an electric mixer. Add 1 cup butter, the sugar, milk, eggs, orange juice concentrate, orange zest, vanilla, cinnamon, nutmeg and cloves and mix well. Spoon into a buttered casserole. Sprinkle evenly with the pecan mixture. Bake at 350 degrees for 30 to 45 minutes.

*Yield: 10 to 12 servings*

# Roasted Whole Pumpkin with Wild Mushroom Bread Pudding

*This recipe is so good. It came to me through Kathy Alex, who hosts "Cooking with Friends" in Grasse, France.*

1 (4-pound) pumpkin, or
  8 small acorn squash
1/4 cup (1/2 stick) butter,
  softened
1 tablespoon thyme
Salt and pepper to taste
Wild Mushroom Bread
  Pudding (below)
1 cup (4 ounces) shredded
  Gruyère or Swiss cheese
Olive oil for brushing

Cut a lid from the top of the pumpkin and scoop out the seeds with a large spoon, scraping the side to remove the fibers. Place the pumpkin in a roasting pan. Spread the butter over the inside of the pumpkin and sprinkle the inside evenly with the thyme. Season with salt and pepper. Fill the pumpkin with Wild Mushroom Bread Pudding and top with the cheese. Replace the lid and brush the entire outer surface with olive oil. Bake at 350 degrees for 1 1/2 hours or until the pumpkin is tender when pierced with a knife.

*Yield: 8 servings*

# Wild Mushroom Bread Pudding

2 large shallots, finely
  chopped
1/2 cup olive oil
2 garlic cloves, finely
  chopped
1 1/2 pounds mixed wild
  mushrooms, chopped
Salt and pepper to taste
1 pound brioche or egg
  bread, cut into cubes,
  dried overnight
1 3/4 cups milk
1 cup stock
1/4 cup mixed chopped fresh
  parsley and thyme

Sautè the shallots in the olive oil in a large skillet until translucent. Add the garlic, mushrooms, salt and pepper and mix well. Cook until the vegetables are tender and the liquid has evaporated, stirring frequently. Remove to a bowl. Add the brioche, milk, stock, parsley and thyme and mix well.

## Pumpkins

*People use pumpkins for decorative purposes these days in numerous ways. Here are just a few examples:*

*As a "bowl" to hold a floral arrangement.*

*As part of a Halloween arrangement at doorways, often used as one of several pumpkins in varying sizes.*

*As a tureen, to hold a large amount of soup. In some cases, smaller pumpkins are hollowed out and used as a bowl for individual servings of stews.*

*Very small pumpkins, as well as larger ones, can be painted with faces to add a touch of humor to party decorations.*

*Martha Stewart suggests that you hollow out a medium pumpkin, line it with plastic and use the pumpkin as a candy dish when trick-or-treaters come calling.*

# Cranberry Chutney

1 (12-ounce) package fresh
    cranberries
2 cups sugar
1 cup water
1 cup orange juice
1 cup golden raisins
1 cup chopped walnuts or
    pecans
1 cup chopped celery
1 medium apple, chopped
1 tablespoon grated orange
    zest
1 teaspoon ginger

Combine the cranberries, sugar, water and orange juice in a 3-quart saucepan and mix well. Bring to a boil, stirring constantly. Reduce the heat. Simmer for 15 minutes, stirring occasionally. Remove from the heat. Add the raisins, walnuts, celery, apple, orange zest and ginger and mix well. Set aside to cool. Chill, covered, until serving time.

*Yield: 8 servings*

*With all of the calories going on in dressing and pumpkin pie, etc., Green Things can provide a delicious escape hatch for those who are stalwart enough to stick to lower calories during the holidays. These are all done the day before, arranged on a glass or china platter (not metal), covered with plastic wrap, and chilled. The olive oil and herbs are in keeping with a healthy diet, too.*

# Green Things

1 cup olive oil or vegetable
    oil, or 1/2 cup of each
Juice of 1 small lemon
    (about 2 tablespoons)
3 tablespoons balsamic
    vinegar
1 teaspoon salt
4 zucchini, julienned
1 tablespoon olive oil
1 bunch broccoli, cut into
    florets, cooked tender-
    crisp
2 bunches asparagus,
    trimmed, cooked tender-
    crisp
1 pint brussels sprouts,
    cut into halves, steamed
Salt and pepper to taste

Combine 1 cup olive oil, the lemon juice, balsamic vinegar and 1 teaspoon salt in a jar with a tight-fitting lid and shake well. Sauté the zucchini in 1 tablespoon olive oil in a skillet just until tender-crisp. Arrange the zucchini, broccoli, asparagus and brussels sprouts on a platter in a pattern that resembles the spokes of a wheel. Drizzle the warm vegetables with 2 tablespoons of the vinaigrette. Chill, covered, overnight. Serve with the remaining vinaigrette on the side in a small cruet with a top. Season with salt and pepper. Garnish with fresh basil, rosemary or tarragon.

*Yield: 12 to 15 servings*

# Pumpkin Pie

1 (29-ounce) can solid-pack
  pumpkin
2 cups sugar
4 eggs, lightly beaten
1/2 teaspoon salt
1 tablespoon vanilla extract
1/2 cup (1 stick) butter,
  melted
2/3 cup half-and-half
1/2 cup milk
Perfect Pie Crust (below)
Caramel Pecan Sauce
  (at right)

Combine the pumpkin, sugar, eggs, salt,
vanilla, butter, half-and-half and milk in a large
bowl and mix until smooth. Pour into Perfect
Pie Crust shells. Bake at 350 degrees for
45 minutes or until the filling is set. Cool on
a wire rack. Spoon Caramel Pecan Sauce over
the top of each serving.

*Yield: 12 to 15 servings*

# Perfect Pie Crust

2 cups flour
1/2 teaspoon salt
3/4 cup (1 1/2 sticks) cold
  unsalted butter
1/4 cup ice water

Combine the flour and salt in a food processor
and process for a few seconds. Add the butter
and process until the mixture resembles coarse
meal. Add the ice water gradually, processing
briefly until the dough begins to hold together.
Divide the dough into 2 equal portions. Wrap
each portion in plastic wrap and chill for
30 minutes or longer. Roll the dough and fit
into two 9-inch pie plates, trimming and
fluting the edges.

## Caramel Pecan Sauce

5 tablespoons dark brown
  sugar
1/4 cup (1/2 stick) butter
5 tablespoons cream
1/2 cup toasted chopped
  pecans

Combine the brown sugar,
butter and cream in a
small saucepan. Cook over
medium heat for 3 to
4 minutes or until the
brown sugar is dissolved
and the butter is melted,
stirring constantly. Remove
from the heat to cool. Stir
in the pecans. This sauce is
also great served over ice
cream or pound cake.

# To Dos & Tah Dahs

# Menus

*A Merry Merry Christmas Feast*

*A Holiday Open House*

*A Tea Party for Any Occasion*

*An Engagement "To Do"*

*A Wedding Reception*

"To Dos" and "Tah Dahs" are for a lot of folks. A big "Tah Dah" would be the Decatur General Foundation Gala or the Pact Ball. These events are very formal and a very elegant menu is planned.

A holiday open house could be formal or informal, but is generally formal with the dining table laden with pickup foods, with punch or drinks served in another room. Small plates and forks may be provided but are not necessary. Cocktail napkins will be placed on the table. Guests mingle, standing up, during the time specified on the invitation and are free to come and go. You can entertain large numbers at a function such as this. This is a "To Do" or a "Tah Dah."

Tea parties held in celebration of any occasion are definitely "To Dos" or "Tah Dahs." Tea parties have always been held in the South for brides, but now they are very popular for birthdays, anniversaries, or just as a "reason for a party." I love tea party food preparation. I remember back to my childhood, my mother and my favorite aunties, Maggie and Dinks, hustling around in the kitchen assisted by me and our maid Effie ("help" was very inexpensive—$5.00 a day) preparing tiny ribbon sandwiches, mints, and scones for small tea parties.

Engagement parties and wedding receptions are indeed "To Dos" and "Tah Dahs." You may prefer to plan the menus for these events and hire a caterer. Having been a caterer, I, of course, insist on preparing food for my "Tah Dahs." Our daughter Lisa and Paul Wallace's reception was at our home with 500 guests and it was when I owned Johnston Street Cafe. I, of course, planned the menu and the staff prepared the food with my help.

This is a funny story about "catering." Bill and I were at a "Tah Dah," at the Grand Hotel in Point Clear, Alabama, while attending the state orthopaedic meeting. I felt I needed to call home to see about the children staying with my parents, and I picked up the phone and said, "I need to call Decatur," to the operator. I thought she had connected me with the outside operator when someone said, "May I help you, ma'am?" I said, "I am trying to call Decatur." Promptly the voice said, "Ma'am, I *am* de Caterer."

# A Merry Merry Christmas Feast

*Curry Dip* • *White Cheddar Biscuits*
*Assorted Lettuce, Pear and Candied Walnut Salad*
*Beef Wellington* • *Creamed Spinach*
*Baby Potatoes with Parsley and Lemon Butter*
*Refrigerator Rolls* • *Chocolate Amaretto Trifle* • *Easy Chocolate Cake*

'Tis the season you eagerly await all year round—the time to get together with loved ones, celebrate the holidays, and remember what is meaningful. This feast is fabulous for Christmas, but is equally wonderful for any special occasion. The table decorations I used with this included a collection I have had for years of crystal angels, crystal candlesticks, white candles, and a bit of Jackson vine, of course, tucked in around these objects. Set your table. Make White Cheddar Biscuits a week early. Freeze in sealable plastic bags. Most of this menu may be prepared the day before. The salad greens may be washed and stored in baggies in the refrigerator, unless of course you are using already prepared lettuces; the candied walnuts sautéed a day ahead and stored in airtight container. Pears, peeled, sliced, and held in orange juice to keep them from turning brown. Scallions chopped, vinaigrette mixed and stored in refrigerator. Oil may be beaten in at the last minute. Potatoes are so simple—they're not even peeled. Creamed spinach may be made a day ahead, refrigerated and reheated the day of. For the Beef Wellington—make your duxelles, cool, and refrigerate the day before. Early afternoon the day of your dinner—sear your beef on all sides. Put aside to cool on paper towels. Proceed to wrap in pastry two or three hours ahead. You may refrigerate until 1 hour or so before completing the cooking. The trifle in its entirety may be prepared the day before and refrigerated. Serve in small bowls or flat champagne glasses. Most of this menu was published in *Southern Lady* magazine, the holiday issue 2001.

# Curry Dip

*This is Shirley McCrary's delicious dip.*

24 ounces cream cheese,
　softened
1 (10-ounce) jar Bengal hot
　chutney
1 (10-ounce) jar mango
　chutney
1 (8-ounce) can crushed
　pineapple, drained
1 (2-ounce) jar candied
　ginger, finely chopped
3 tablespoons curry powder
1 tablespoon garlic powder
1 cup sour cream
1 (11-ounce) can cashews

Beat the cream cheese in a mixing bowl until smooth. Add the Bengal hot chutney, mango chutney, pineapple, candied ginger, curry powder, garlic powder and sour cream and mix well. Sprinkle the cashews over the top. Serve with pita chips for dipping. May soften the candied ginger in a small amount of the drained pineapple juice in a bowl if desired. Serve with tiny whole wheat crackers if you prefer..

*Yield: 30 servings*

# White Cheddar Biscuits

1 1/2 cups flour
1/2 teaspoon white pepper
8 ounces aged white
　Cheddar cheese, shredded
1/3 cup margarine
1 egg, lightly beaten
40 pecan halves

Combine the flour and white pepper in a bowl and mix well. Cut in the cheese and margarine until the mixture resembles coarse crumbs. Stir in the egg and shape the mixture into a ball. Knead briefly until well combined. Shape the dough into a log 7 inches long and 2 inches in diameter. Chill, wrapped in plastic wrap, for 2 hours or longer. Cut the log into 1/8-inch-thick slices. Arrange 1 inch apart on an ungreased baking sheet; reshape if necessary. Press 1 pecan half into each slice. Bake at 400 degrees for 8 to 10 minutes or until the bottoms and edges are light brown. Remove to a wire rack to cool.

*Yield: 40 biscuits*

# Assorted Lettuce, Pear and Candied Walnut Salad

1/2 cup chopped walnuts
3 tablespoons brown sugar
2 tablespoons butter
Mixed salad greens such as romaine, leaf lettuce and Boston lettuce
1 firm ripe pear (Bosc or Bartlett)
3 scallions, chopped
3 to 4 ounces crumbled bleu cheese
Balsamic Vinaigrette (below)

Sauté the walnuts and brown sugar in the butter in a heavy skillet over medium heat until the walnuts begin to soften. Remove to a bowl to cool. Rinse and drain the salad greens. Tear into bite-size pieces and place in a large bowl. Core and chop the pear just before serving. Add the pear, scallions, candied walnuts and cheese to the salad and toss to mix. Pour Balsamic Vinaigrette over the salad and toss to mix. Serve immediately.

*Yield: 4 to 6 servings*

## Balsamic Vinaigrette

1 teaspoon dry mustard
1/2 teaspoon seasoned salt
1/4 teaspoon freshly ground pepper
3 tablespoons balsamic vinegar
2 tablespoons sugar
1/2 teaspoon onion juice
1 garlic clove, crushed
3/4 cup olive oil

Combine the dry mustard, seasoned salt and pepper in a bowl and mix well. Add the vinegar, sugar, onion juice and garlic and mix well. Let stand for 1 hour. Pour the mixture through a wire-mesh strainer into a bowl, discarding the solids. Add the olive oil in a fine stream, whisking constantly until blended.

## Frosted Fruits

*Mix one egg white with a fork in a bowl until frothy. Brush onto desired fruits, such as grapes, plums, crab apples, pears and apples. Roll fruits in sugar or sift on sugar. Set on a wire rack to dry.*

*This makes a beautiful centerpiece mounded on a silver cake pedestal and adorned with a big gold bow and gold ribbon curled down the table.*

## Blush Cream Sauce

1 cup red wine
1 tablespoon minced shallots
1 tablespoon chopped fresh thyme
5 white peppercorns
1 bay leaf
1 quart heavy cream
Salt and white pepper to taste

Combine the wine, shallots, thyme, peppercorns and bay leaf in a large skillet and mix well. Cook over medium heat until almost all of the liquid has evaporated, stirring occasionally. Add the cream and simmer until thickened, stirring occasionally. Strain through a fine sieve into a medium bowl. Season with salt and pepper.

1 (6- to 8-pound) beef tenderloin, trimmed, at room temperature
1/4 cup olive oil
Salt and pepper
Duxelles (below)
1 (16-ounce) package puff pastry
1 egg, beaten
1 tablespoon water
Blush Cream Sauce (at left)

1/2 cup (1 stick) butter
2 shallots, minced
1 pound mushrooms, minced
1 tablespoon chopped fresh thyme, or 1 teaspoon dried thyme
Salt to taste

# Beef Wellington

Sear the beef tenderloin on all sides in the olive oil in a large skillet for a total of 5 minutes; cool. Sprinkle with salt and pepper. Turn the tapered end of the tenderloin under itself and secure with a wooden pick. Spread a 1/4-inch-thick layer of Duxelles evenly over the top of the tenderloin. Roll out the puff pastry and wrap around the tenderloin, encasing completely and pinching the overlapped edges together to seal. Place seam side down on a foil- or parchment paper-lined baking sheet. Decorate the top with additional pastry cut into star shapes if desired. Mix the egg and water in a small bowl. Brush the pastry lightly with 1/2 of the egg wash. Let stand for 5 to 10 minutes to dry. Brush with the remaining egg wash. Bake at 400 degrees for 45 minutes for rare, 50 minutes for medium or 55 minutes for well done. Cool for 10 minutes before slicing. Garnish with fresh rosemary. Serve with Blush Cream Sauce. May place the pastry-covered tenderloin in the refrigerator for 5 minutes if the first application of egg wash does not dry in the specified time.

*Yield: 12 to 14 servings*

## Duxelles

Melt the butter in a heavy skillet over medium-low heat. Add the shallots, mushrooms, thyme and salt and mix well. Cook slowly for 5 minutes or until the mixture is of a paste consistency, stirring occasionally. Cool. May mince the mushrooms in a food processor if desired.

# Creamed Spinach

2 (10-ounce) bags ready-to-
  use fresh spinach, or
  1¹/2 pounds fresh spinach
6 tablespoons butter
¹/4 cup flour
¹/4 cup chopped onion
1 bay leaf
1 whole clove
2 cups half-and-half

Remove any tough stems from the spinach. Cook in a small amount of water to cover in a covered saucepan until wilted. Drain and chop the cooked spinach. Melt the butter in a heavy medium saucepan over medium heat. Add the flour and cook for 2 minutes or until bubbly, stirring constantly. Stir in the onion, bay leaf and clove. Whisk in the half-and-half gradually. Bring the mixture to a boil, whisking constantly. Cook for 5 minutes or until thickened, whisking constantly. Reduce the heat to low and simmer for 5 minutes longer, whisking frequently. The sauce should be very thick. Discard the bay leaf and clove. Add the spinach and stir to mix. May be prepared 1 day ahead, refrigerated and reheated.

*Yield: 4 servings*

# Baby Potatoes with Parsley and Lemon Butter

3 pounds mixed baby
  potatoes (white and red)
Salt to taste
6 tablespoons butter
6 tablespoons chopped
  fresh parsley
1 tablespoon grated lemon
  zest
1 tablespoon fresh lemon
  juice
1¹/2 teaspoons salt
¹/2 teaspoon pepper

Scrub and rinse the potatoes thoroughly. Cook the potatoes in a large pot of salted boiling water to cover for 20 minutes or until tender; drain. May be prepared 2 hours ahead. Let stand at room temperature. Melt the butter in a large heavy skillet over medium-high heat. Add the potatoes, 4 tablespoons of the parsley, the lemon zest, lemon juice, 1¹/2 teaspoons salt and the pepper. Cook for 5 minutes or until the potatoes are heated through and beginning to brown, tossing frequently. Remove to a bowl. Sprinkle with the remaining parsley and serve.

*Yield: 6 servings*

# Refrigerator Rolls

*This recipe is Sandy Nix's recipe, first printed in* Cotton Country Cooking.
*I cut down on the amount of sugar. We mixed this times twenty
at Johnston Street Cafe.*

1 cup water
1/2 cup (1 stick) butter or
   margarine
1/2 cup shortening
2/3 cup sugar
1 1/2 teaspoons salt
1 cup warm water
   (105 to 115 degrees)
2 envelopes dry yeast
2 eggs, lightly beaten
6 cups (about) flour

Microwave 1 cup water in a 2-quart microwave-safe dish on High until boiling. Add the butter and shortening and stir until melted. Add the sugar and salt and mix well. Cool to lukewarm. Pour 1 cup warm water into an electric mixer bowl. Sprinkle with the yeast and stir to dissolve. Add the butter mixture and eggs and beat well. Add enough of the flour to make a thick dough, mixing thoroughly. Place the dough in a ceramic bowl and chill, covered, overnight. Roll the dough 1/4 inch thick on a floured surface 2 1/2 hours before serving time. Cut the dough with a round biscuit cutter and fold each roll in half. Arrange on a greased baking sheet. Brush with melted butter. Let rise for 1 1/2 hours. Bake at 400 degrees for 12 to 13 minutes or until done. May bake these ahead. Cool and freeze.

*Yield: 36 rolls*

# Chocolate Amaretto Trifle

Easy Chocolate Cake
  (below), without frosting
1/2 cup amaretto
Custard (at right)
2 cups whipping cream,
  whipped
1 cup sliced almonds,
  toasted

Crumble the prepared Easy Chocolate Cake in a medium bowl and drizzle with the amaretto. Layer the amaretto mixture, Custard, whipped cream and almonds 1/3 at a time in a trifle bowl. Pipe additional whipped cream decoratively over the top if desired. Garnish with chocolate covered coffee beans.

*Yield: 20 to 25 servings*

# Easy Chocolate Cake

1 cup boiling water
4 ounces unsweetened
  chocolate
1/2 cup (1 stick) butter
2 cups cake flour, sifted
1/2 teaspoon salt
1 teaspoon baking soda
2 cups sugar
1/2 cup buttermilk
2 eggs
1 teaspoon vanilla extract

Pour the boiling water over the chocolate and butter in a large mixing bowl and stir until melted and smooth; cool. Sift the cake flour, salt, baking soda and sugar into the bowl and beat for 2 minutes. Add the buttermilk and beat for 2 minutes. Add the eggs and vanilla and beat for 2 minutes. Pour into a greased and floured 9×13-inch cake pan. Bake at 325 degrees for 30 minutes. Cool in the pan on a wire rack. Frost as desired or use for trifle.

*Yield: 10 servings*

## Custard

1/2 cup sugar
1/2 teaspoon salt
2 1/2 tablespoons
  cornstarch
2 1/2 cups milk
4 egg yolks, beaten
1 teaspoon vanilla extract

Combine the sugar, salt and cornstarch in a 2-quart microwave-safe glass measuring cup and mix well. Whisk in the milk gradually. Microwave on High for 8 minutes or until slightly thickened, stirring at 2-minute intervals. Whisk in the egg yolks until well blended. Microwave on Medium-High for 1 minute longer, stir and cool. Stir in the vanilla. This custard is so easy to make in the microwave. Use this custard for banana pudding too.

*Yield: (about) 4 cups*

# A Holiday Open House

*Holiday Punch* • *Shrimp and Salsa Mousse*
*Oven-Baked Crab Dip* • *Cranberry Chutney over Brie (page 122)*
*Parmesan Mushrooms with Grapes*
*Asparagus in the Pink* • *Asparagus in the White*
*Beef Tenderloin with Horseradish Sauce and Cheese Herb Biscuits*
*Chocolate Orange Truffles*
*Candied Citrus Peel*

Christmas has always been a glorious holiday, a celebration of Jesus' birth, but also a celebration with family and friends, bringing everyone together to feast and celebrate. What better time when our houses are all decorated to host an open house. It does require a lot of preparation, but so many things can be done ahead and frozen. Lisa and Paul Wallace, our daughter and son-in-law hosted a Christmas Open House recently a few days before Christmas in the evening. Paul's parents, Beth and Bill Wallace, host a "Christmas Wassailing" Open House in the afternoon, on Sunday, earlier in the month. Lisa's menu lends itself to advance preparation. The chutney and the toast points can be made many days ahead. The sauce for the asparagus and the blanching of the asparagus can be done the day before, as can the mushrooms, which can be refrigerated unbaked. The horseradish sauce lends itself to be made a day ahead. The orange truffles freeze well and can be made anytime. Assemble all of your silver or most festive platters and trays and place them on your holiday table, labeling each so there will be no confusion when you begin filling them. Small cocktail napkins and small crystal plates may also be placed early. Forks are not a necessity since all of the food is finger food. Punch can be made the day before and stored in gallon jugs or a large picnic thermos. Alcohol, if used, should be added to the punch just before the guests arrive. Be sure that you have plenty of ice on hand. Generally Lisa uses a wreath on her table with candlelight. Another great Christmas table decoration is the crystallized fruit on a cake pedestal, with ribbons. Baked crab meat may be made a day ahead and refrigerated. The day of your party, check all supplies, do last minute sprucing up, and an hour or so before guests arrive, start arranging your food on platters. Have plenty of garnishes such as flowers and herbs. Plan to elevate some of the food for interesting presentation.

# Holiday Punch

4 cups cranberry juice
1 1/2 cups sugar
4 cups pineapple juice
1 tablespoon almond extract
2 quarts ginger ale, chilled

Combine the cranberry juice, sugar, pineapple juice and almond extract in a large bowl and stir until the sugar is dissolved. Pour into sealable plastic freezer bags and freeze until solid. Thaw until slushy and pour into a punch bowl. Add the ginger ale and stir to mix.

*Yield: 20 servings*

# Shrimp and Salsa Mousse

2 tablespoons unflavored gelatin
1/2 cup cold water
1 1/2 cups boiling water
16 ounces cream cheese, softened
2 cups medium salsa
1 cup mayonnaise
1 (4-ounce) can small shrimp, drained
8 ounces cooked crab meat, flaked

Soften the gelatin in the cold water in a small heatproof bowl. Place the bowl in a larger heatproof bowl filled with the boiling water. Let stand until the gelatin is dissolved, stirring occasionally. Combine the cream cheese, salsa, mayonnaise and gelatin mixture in a food processor and process until well blended. Remove to a bowl. Fold in the shrimp and crab meat. Spoon into a plastic wrap-lined mold. Chill, covered, until firm. Unmold onto a serving plate. Serve with Bremner Wafers.

*Yield: 50 servings*

*Add ice cubes made from additional pineapple juice or place an ice mold in the punch bowl. May thaw punch in the microwave if pressed for time.*

# Oven-Baked Crab Dip

*This may be frozen in unbaked stage for as long as a month.*

16 ounces cream cheese,
  softened
1/3 cup mayonnaise
1 tablespoon confectioners'
  sugar
1 tablespoon chablis or dry
  white wine
1/2 teaspoon onion juice
1/2 teaspoon prepared
  mustard
1/4 teaspoon garlic salt
1/4 teaspoon salt
6 ounces fresh crab meat,
  flaked or 1 (6-ounce) can
  lump crab meat, drained,
  flaked
Chopped fresh parsley

Combine the cream cheese, mayonnaise, confectioners' sugar, chablis, onion juice, prepared mustard, garlic salt and salt in a bowl and mix well. Stir in the crab meat gently. Spoon into a lightly greased 1-quart baking dish. Bake at 375 degrees for 15 minutes. Sprinkle with parsley. Serve with toast points or melba toast rounds. May double to make 50 servings.

*Yield: 25 servings*

*We used this recipe for crab dip so much at Johnston Street Cafe for catered affairs. I am sure we prepared a ton of it over the ten years we were in business.*

# Parmesan Mushrooms with Grapes

20 fresh medium
  mushrooms
20 seedless green grapes
2 (5-ounce) packages herb
  and garlic cheese,
  softened
1/2 cup (1 stick) unsalted
  butter, melted
1 cup grated Parmesan
  cheese
Freshly ground pepper

Remove the stems from the mushrooms and reserve for another use. Place 1 grape in each mushroom cap. Mound 1 1/2 teaspoons of the herb and garlic cheese over each mushroom, completely enclosing the grape. Dip each mushroom in the butter and roll in the Parmesan cheese to coat. Reserve any cheese that does not adhere. Place the mushrooms in an ungreased 10×15-inch baking pan. Chill, covered, for 20 minutes. Bake at 400 degrees for 15 minutes. Sprinkle with the reserved Parmesan cheese and pepper. May use a Silpat or parchment paper-lined baking sheet. Triple the recipe to serve 50.

*Yield: 20 servings*

# Asparagus in the Pink

3 pounds fresh asparagus,
  trimmed
3 cups mayonnaise
2 (4-ounce) jars roasted
  pimentos
1/2 teaspoon cayenne pepper

Cook the asparagus in boiling water to cover in a saucepan for 7 minutes, or less for pencil asparagus. Drain in a colander; cover with ice. Let stand until cool. Drain on paper towels. Combine the mayonnaise, pimentos and cayenne pepper in a food processor and process for 1 minute. Put sauce into a brandy snifter or crystal glass in the center of a round crystal or silver tray. Arrange some of the asparagus in the snifter or glass, making sure the tips of the asparagus flair outward. Arrange the remaining asparagus in a spoke pattern at the base of the snifter.

*Yield: 30 servings*

# Asparagus in the White

3 pounds fresh asparagus,
  trimmed
2 cups sour cream
2/3 cup mayonnaise
1/2 cup chopped scallions
3 tablespoons plus 1
  teaspoon drained capers
4 teaspoons tarragon
2 teaspoons sugar
2 teaspoons thyme
1 teaspoon garlic salt
1 1/2 teaspoons freshly
  ground pepper

Cook the asparagus in boiling water to cover in a saucepan for 7 minutes, or less for pencil asparagus. Drain in a colander and cover with ice. Let stand until cool. Drain on paper towels. Combine the sour cream, mayonnaise, scallions, capers, tarragon, sugar, thyme, garlic salt and pepper in a food processor and process for 1 minute. Serve the asparagus with the white sauce. May arrange as in above recipe in a brandy snifter.

*Yield: 30 servings*

*Serve asparagus within 3 hours of cooking or chill, covered, in layers separated by paper towels in a storage container for as long as 2 days.*

# Beef Tenderloin with Whipped Horseradish Sauce

1 quart whipping cream
1 cup prepared horseradish sauce
1 cup shredded white horseradish
1 tablespoon sugar
2 tablespoons wine vinegar
1 large onion, sliced
3 beef tenderloins, skinned, cleaned
Vegetable oil
Vermouth
Salt and cracked pepper

Whip the cream in a mixing bowl until stiff. Fold in the prepared horseradish sauce, shredded white horseradish, sugar and vinegar. Chill, covered, until serving time. Scatter the onion over the bottom of a roasting pan. Arrange the tenderloins over the top. Combine the desired amount of oil and vermouth in a bowl and mix well. Brush over the tenderloins. Season generously with salt and cracked pepper. Roast at 400 degrees for 45 minutes for medium-rare or until done to taste. Slice thinly and serve on Cheese Herb Biscuits (below) with the whipped horseradish sauce.

*Yield: 50 servings*

*Ann Pollard, a great cook and friend, helped me organize Johnston Street Cafe and worked with me for two years before she opened her own restaurant, The Green Bottle Grill, in Huntsville. This beef tenderloin is from her files.*

# Cheese Herb Biscuits

2 cups flour
1 tablespoon baking powder
1 teaspoon salt
1/4 cup shortening, chilled
3/4 cup shredded Gruyère cheese
1/4 cup chopped fresh dillweed
1 cup milk
2 tablespoons unsalted butter, melted

Combine the flour, baking powder and salt in a food processor and pulse to mix. Add the shortening and process until crumbly. Remove to a medium bowl. Stir in the cheese and dillweed. Add the milk, stirring until a soft dough forms that pulls away from the side of the bowl. Knead on a lightly floured surface just until the dough is mixed. Roll 1/2 inch thick. Cut with a floured heart-shaped cutter. Arrange on an ungreased baking sheet. Brush with the melted butter. Bake at 450 degrees for 12 to 15 minutes or until golden brown.

*Yield: 12 to 14 biscuits*

# Chocolate Orange Truffles

1/4 cup (1/2 stick) butter, cut
   into small pieces
1/3 cup whipping cream
7 ounces semisweet
   chocolate, chopped
1 egg yolk
1 teaspoon grated orange
   zest
2 tablespoons Grand
   Marnier (optional)
Baking cocoa or finely
   chopped pecans

Combine the butter and cream in a small saucepan. Cook over low heat until the butter melts and the cream bubbles around the edge, stirring occasionally. Remove from the heat. Add the chocolate. Let stand, covered, until the chocolate melts. Stir until smooth. Stir in the egg yolk. Add the orange zest and Grand Marnier and mix well. Chill until firm. Roll into 1-inch balls. Roll in baking cocoa or chopped pecans to coat. May microwave the butter, cream and chocolate in a microwave-safe dish on Medium until melted. Stir until smooth. Proceed as above.

*Yield: 4 to 6 servings*

# Candied Citrus Peel

Citrus fruit such as oranges,
   grapefruit, lemons or
   limes
2 cups sugar
1/2 cup water

Remove the zest only from the citrus fruit using a "stripper" or very sharp knife. Do not peel off any of the bitter white pith. Blanch the strips in boiling water in a bowl for a few seconds before proceeding. Combine the sugar and water in a small heavy saucepan. Bring to a boil; reduce the heat. Add the citrus strips and simmer for 40 minutes. Cover the pan. The condensation will run down the side of the pan and help to dissolve the sugar on the side. Cool the mixture in the pan. Remove the citrus strips to waxed paper or foil to harden. May be stored, tightly covered, in the freezer indefinitely. May stir 2 tablespoons orange-flavored liqueur, such as Cointreau, Grand Marnier or Triple Sec into the syrup after removing from the heat.

*Yield: variable*

# A Tea Party for Any Occasion

*Champagne • Tea • Mocha Punch*
*Cucumber Rounds • Cheese Straws*
*Johnston Street Cafe Chicken Salad (page 55) in Chou Puff Pastry*
*Heart-Shaped Scones with Mock Devonshire Cream*
*Asparagus Roll-Ups • Confetti Stuffed Pecans*
*Catherine's Brownies • Raspberry Brownies*
*Lemon Curd in Chocolate Cordial Cups*

A tea party is one of the most delightful of all occasions. They are becoming more and more popular, as they may be held in celebration of any occasion—wedding reception, birthday celebration, baby shower, and wedding shower—and done informally or formally. Afternoon tea traditionally begins with a selection of dainty tea sandwiches and small pastries. One of the most enjoyable activities that I have had in the last several years is having a tea party in Atlanta with our oldest daughter, Libby, and her friend, Jane Jordan. We have many stories to tell of these affairs, but it has been a time of real togetherness which we share preparing for this occasion. I arrive in Atlanta the day before our Sunday afternoon party laden down with all sorts of goodies that I have prepared and frozen in the last month. Pastries do not freeze well over a month. We generally spend the night before the party arranging flowers and making tea sandwich ingredients. There is always an open invitation to special friends, like Beverly Douglas, who want to assist in the preparation. The morning of, we cut sandwich breads and spread with onion cream cheese for the cucumber rounds. Moisten and wring out paper towels or tea towels for placing over sandwiches to keep them moist. Refrigerate. One of the very popular items, the confetti pecans, may be stuffed and refrigerated the morning of. The brownies and lemon curd can all be made several days ahead and and the brownies may be frozen. Lemon curd will keep three weeks in the refrigerator. Carl, Libby's husband, is a "dear" as he is constantly "on call" to run to the grocery to grab an item we've forgotten or to tend Alex while we are busy getting things ready. He is the greatest. At the last minute we prepare the tea, place pastries, brownies, etc. on serving trays. Place the flutes on a silver tray for the Champagne. Several prizes are given for the best ensemble. Everyone wears hats, gloves, etc. There is a lot of mingling and no one wants to leave. How special!

# Mocha Punch

*This mocha punch could be used for a bridal shower. It is delicious and was shared with me by Marietta Robison, who is a sweet lady and an excellent cook and teacher.*

1 cup boiling water
1 cup sugar
3 tablespoons instant coffee
   crystals
1/2 gallon chocolate ice
   cream, softened
1/2 gallon vanilla ice cream,
   softened
2 quarts milk

Combine the boiling water, sugar and coffee crystals in a bowl and mix well. Chill, covered, until serving time. May be prepared several days ahead. Combine the chocolate ice cream and vanilla ice cream in a punch bowl. Add the milk and the coffee syrup and stir until creamy.

*Yield: 1 1/2 gallons*

# Cucumber Rounds

Cucumbers, thinly sliced
White bread
Boursin Cheese Spread
   (page 38)

Cover the desired number of unpeeled cucumber slices with ice water in a large bowl. Drain and pat dry with paper towels just before preparing sandwiches. Cut rounds from white bread with a biscuit cutter. Spread each round with Boursin Cheese Spread and place 1 cucumber slice on top. Arrange on a serving tray and cover with dampened paper towels to prevent the sandwiches from drying out. Chill, covered, until ready to serve.

*Yield: variable*

## A Perfect Cup of Tea

*To make a perfect cup of tea, first fill the kettle with fresh water. Bring the water to a rolling boil in the kettle. Meanwhile, warm a clean tea pot by rinsing it with hot water. Place 1 teaspoon of tea per person and 1 extra for the "pot" in the tea pot. Pour the boiling water over the tea. Brew, with the lid on the tea pot, for 3 to 5 minutes. Stir the tea and pour through a strainer before serving.*

*Barbara Griffin, my friend and helper who worked with me at Johnston Street Cafe, has made thousands of these. She is still making them for me. The recipe for Cheese Straws was in* Southern Scrumptious, *but I had to include it here, for you cannot have a tea party without cheese straws. This is the very best recipe for cheese straws the South can offer. Frances Patrick, our daughter Libby's mother-in-law, shared this one with me. I was thrilled that the cholesterol level could be reduced by substituting corn oil margarine for butter in this recipe.*

# Cheese Straws

16 ounces New York State
    extra-sharp Cheddar
    cheese, shredded
2 cups corn oil margarine,
    softened
4 cups flour
1 tablespoon sugar
3/4 teaspoon cayenne pepper
1/2 teaspoon baking powder
1/8 to 1/4 teaspoon salt

Beat the cheese and margarine in a mixing bowl until blended. Sift the flour, sugar, cayenne pepper, baking powder and salt together. Add to the cheese mixture and mix well. Spoon into a cookie press. Pipe into straws on an ungreased baking sheet. Bake at 350 degrees for 18 minutes or until light brown. Cool on a wire rack. May roll into cylinders about 2 inches in diameter. Chill, covered, or freeze until baking time. Slice and bake as above sprinkled with chopped pecans.

*Yield: 200 cheese straws*

# Chou Puff Pastry

2 cups flour
1/2 teaspoon salt
2 cups water
1 cup (2 sticks) margarine
8 eggs

Mix the flour and salt together. Boil the water and margarine in a saucepan until the margarine melts, stirring constantly. Remove from the heat. Beat in the flour mixture with a metal spoon until blended. Cook over medium heat for 1 minute, stirring constantly. Spoon into a food processor. Add 4 of the eggs and process for 30 seconds. Add the remaining eggs and process for 1 minute. Drop 1/2 of the mixture by teaspoonfuls onto a parchment-lined baking sheet. Bake on the middle oven rack at 425 degrees for 15 minutes. Reduce the oven temperature to 375 degrees. Bake for 5 minutes. Reduce the oven temperature to 350 degrees. Make a slit in the top of each pastry. Bake for 5 minutes. Repeat with the remaining egg mixture. Fill the puffs with savory fillings such as chicken salad, shrimp paste and boursin cheese or with dessert fillings such as lemon curd and white chocolate mousse.

*Yield: 60 small puffs*

# Heart-Shaped Scones

2 1/2 cups flour
1 tablespoon baking powder
1/2 teaspoon salt
1/2 cup (1 stick) butter,
  chopped, chilled
1/4 cup sugar
2/3 cup milk or whipping
  cream
Mock Devonshire Cream
  (page 26)

Mix the flour, baking powder and salt together in a bowl. Cut in the butter with a pastry blender or fork until crumbly. Stir in the sugar. Add the milk, stirring with a fork until a soft dough forms. Shape into a ball. Knead on a lightly floured surface 10 to 12 times. Roll and cut with a heart-shaped cutter. Arrange on an ungreased baking sheet. Bake at 425 degrees for 12 minutes. Remove to a wire rack to cool. Arrange on a serving platter. Serve with Mock Devonshire Cream and your favorite jam in small crystal bowls.

*Yield: 40 small scones*

# Asparagus Roll-Ups

8 slices bacon, crisp-cooked,
  crumbled
8 ounces cream cheese,
  softened
12 thin slices white bread,
  crusts removed
12 asparagus spears, cooked,
  chilled
Melted butter

Combine the bacon and cream cheese in a bowl and mix well. Roll the bread slices flat with a rolling pin. Spread the bacon mixture evenly over the bread slices. Arrange 1 asparagus spear in the center of each slice. Roll to enclose. Arrange on a baking sheet seam side down. Chill, covered, until serving time. Brush with melted butter and broil until light brown. Serve hot. May slice rolls into 1/4- to 1/2-inch rounds and broil until brown on each side.

*Yield: 10 to 15 servings*

## Tea for Large Parties

*Making tea by the classic method may well be impractical if you're preparing tea for a large group. It's easier to use the following tea concentrate, developed by the Tea Council of the U.S.A., to give an excellent cup of tea with all the full flavor of a fresh-brewed cup. The recipe makes enough for about 25 servings.*

Make tea as usual, but use 1 quart (4 cups) of water over 2/3 cup of tea leaves. Let stand 5 minutes, then stir and strain into a teapot or pitcher. When ready to serve, pour about 2 tablespoons of concentrate into each cup, then fill cup with steaming hot water.

## Favorite Teas

Earl Grey—The original scented with Bergamot

Darjeeling—From high in the Himalayas—stimulating

Oolong —The Formosan "Champagne of Teas"—fragrance of peach

Winey Keemun - Classic English Breakfast Tea with unusual depth

Connoisseur—A masterful blend from many origins, balanced

Lapsang Souchong—Hand fired with exotic woods

Jasmine—Blossoms and tea leaves, dried and left almost green

# Confetti Stuffed Pecans

40 large pecan halves
16 ounces cream cheese softened
1 (8-ounce) can crushed pineapple, well drained
1/3 cup orange marmalade
3 tablespoons ginger chutney
1/2 cup finely chopped pecans
1/4 cup finely chopped green bell pepper
1 tablespoon minced onion
1/2 teaspoon celery salt
1/2 teaspoon onion salt
8 maraschino cherries, finely chopped

Spread the pecan halves in a single layer on a baking sheet with no added salt or oil. Roast at 250 degrees for 45 minutes; cool. Beat the cream cheese in a mixing bowl until smooth. Add the pineapple, orange marmalade, chutney, chopped pecans, bell pepper, onion, celery salt, onion salt and cherries and mix well. Pipe or mound 1 scant teaspoon of the cream cheese mixture onto each of 20 pecan halves, flat side up. Top each with a remaining pecan half, flat side down.

*Yield: 20 stuffed pecans*

# Lemon Curd in Chocolate Cordial Cups

*Cordial cups may be found in specialty shops.*

1/2 cup unsalted butter
1 1/2 cups sugar
4 eggs
Juice of 3 lemons
1 1/2 teaspoons grated lemon peel
60 Belgium chocolate cordial cups

Microwave the butter on High in a 2-quart Pyrex cup just until melted. Add the sugar, eggs, lemon juice and lemon peel and stir until blended. Microwave on High for 4 minutes, whisking at 2 minute intervals. Microwave on Medium-High for 4 minutes, whisking at 2 minute intervals. Continue to microwave until thickened. Let stand until cool. Refrigerate, covered, until ready to use. Spoon 1 teaspoon of the lemon curd into each cordial cup.

*Yield: 60 servings*

# Catherine's Brownies

1 1/4 cups sifted flour
1 teaspoon salt
1/2 teaspoon baking powder
1 cup (2 sticks) unsalted
   butter or margarine,
   softened
2 cups sugar
4 eggs
4 ounces unsweetened
   chocolate, melted
1 1/2 teaspoons vanilla extract
1 to 2 cups chopped nuts
Confectioners' sugar

Sift the flour, salt and baking powder together. Cream the butter with the sugar and eggs in a mixing bowl until light and fluffy. Beat in the chocolate, vanilla and flour mixture at low speed until well mixed. Stir in the nuts. Pour into 2 greased 8×8-inch baking pans. Bake at 325 degrees for 30 to 35 minutes or until the brownies begin to pull away from the sides of the pans. Cut into small squares while warm. Cool in the pans on a wire rack. Dust with confectioners' sugar.

*Yield: 24 brownies*

# Raspberry Brownies

8 ounces unsweetened
   chocolate
1 cup (2 sticks) butter
1 cup (2 sticks) margarine
4 cups sugar
8 eggs, beaten
2 cups flour
1 teaspoon salt
2 cups chopped pecans
1 1/2 cups raspberry
   preserves
2 cups (12 ounces) chocolate
   chips
1 cup whipping cream

Combine 8 ounces unsweetened chocolate, the butter and margarine in a 2-quart microwave-safe dish. Microwave until melted. Stir until smooth. Combine the sugar and eggs in a bowl and mix well. Stir in the chocolate mixture, flour and salt. Add the pecans and mix well. Spoon into two 9×12-inch baking pans sprayed with nonstick cooking spray. Bake at 350 degrees for 30 minutes; do not overbake. Spread with the preserves. Let stand until cool. Microwave 2 cups chocolate chips in a 2-quart microwave-safe bowl on Medium for 2 minutes or until melted. Add the cream and whisk until smooth. Spread over the cooled brownies. Cut into squares. Refrigerate, covered, until ready to serve.

*Yield: 12 large or 48 small brownies*

*These Raspberry Brownies have become famous. Each time I would go to Neiman Marcus in Atlanta for a book signing and food demo, the epicure director, Biya Kahn, would ask me to bring some of these brownies. I have also taken many, many to Table Matters in Birmingham owned by my cute friend, Patricia Murray. I had to include the recipe in this book.*

# An Engagement "To Do"

*Champagne Punch • Nonalcoholic Fruit Punch • Macadamia Cheese Snaps
Baked Fiesta Spinach Dip • Creamed Chicken Magnolia • Country Ham Cheesecake
Warm Brie with Caramelized Apples • Artichoke Squares • Black-Eyed Pea Relish
Caviar Eggs • Pork Tenderloin with Mustard Caper Sauce served with Sweet Potato Biscuits
Red Potatoes with Gorganzola Cream, Bacon and Pecans • Devil's Fudge*

What Fun! These parties seem to be filled with excitement. Families and friends of the engaged couple come together for an evening of celebrating. Recently, we held a celebration for Lee Worthy, daughter of Jan and Jim, at our home. Lee and Trey Rietch are now happily married. The party was a cocktail buffet with most of the items that we have on this menu. The event began at 7:00 p.m. and we were happy to say that the atmosphere was so warm with all of Decatur and Moulton friends and family congratulating the precious couple. The menu lends itself to much advance preparation if you decide not to hire a caterer. Of course, many of these items could be used for predinner appetizers for other occasions, or for an open house or cocktail buffet. The Macadamia Cheese Snaps are a "snap" to make and can be made a couple of weeks ahead and frozen in an airtight container. The wild mushroom mixture can be prepared the day before, as can the puff pastry squares which can be baked, placed in a sealable plastic bag until the day of the party. The mushroom mixture is warmed, placed on pastry squares and a tray just before serving. The Caviar Eggs should be done the morning of your event. The caper sauce and the rolls for the pork tenderloin can be done ahead. I would bake the tenderloin and boil the potatoes the morning of the party as well as cooking the caramelized apples for the brie. Artichoke Squares actually can be frozen—done a week ahead. If you are attempting to prepare all the food for a party this large, I would have kitchen help or volunteers to help me assemble each item and place on trays, using flowers and herbs to decorate each tray. Elevate some of the food so that it is not all the same level. We used a very large green Italian pottery pitcher with flowers and vines cascading down. Bars were set up in the family room and the terrace to accommodate some of the heavy traffic in the dining room. You could also have food all over the house and on the terrace instead of all of it on the dining table.

# Champagne Punch

3 cups (about) mixed sliced
    fresh strawberries,
    oranges, lemons and
    pineapple
16 to 18 ounces Cognac
1 large block of ice
3 bottles Champagne, chilled
3 cups sparkling water or
    club soda
Maraschino cherry juice
    (optional)

Place the fruit in a large punch bowl. Add the Cognac and ice. Pour the Champagne and sparkling water over the top and stir briefly. Stir in a splash of cherry juice. May triple for a party of 100 guests.

*Yield: 25 to 30 (1/2 cup) servings*

# Nonalcoholic Fruit Punch

2 1/2 cups sugar
1 cup water
2 cups strong brewed tea
1 cup lemon juice
2 1/2 cups orange juice
2 cups pineapple juice
1 quart ginger ale

Combine the sugar and water in a saucepan and mix well. Heat until the sugar dissolves and the mixture is of a syrup consistency, stirring frequently. Let stand to cool. Pour into a punch bowl. Add the tea, lemon juice, orange juice, pineapple juice and enough additional water to measure 1 1/2 gallons and mix well. Add the ginger ale and stir to mix. Garnish with sliced strawberries.

*Yield: 50 servings*

# Macadamia Cheese Snaps

1/4 cup (1/2 stick) butter,
  softened
1 cup baking mix
1 egg, lightly beaten
1 cup macadamia nuts,
  coarsely chopped
1/2 cup (2 ounces) shredded
  sharp Cheddar cheese
Cayenne pepper to taste

Combine the butter and baking mix in a bowl
and mix until crumbly. Stir in the eggs,
macadamia nuts, cheese and cayenne pepper.
Drop by teaspoonfuls onto a greased baking
sheet. Bake at 400 degrees for 8 minutes. Cool
on a wire rack. Store in an airtight container.

*Yield: 35 cheese snaps*

# Baked Fiesta Spinach Dip

1 cup chopped onion
1 tablespoon vegetable oil
1 cup chunky medium salsa,
  well drained
1 (10-ounce) package frozen
  chopped spinach, thawed
2 1/2 cups (10 ounces)
  shredded Monterey Jack
  cheese
8 ounces light cream cheese,
  cubed
1 cup light cream
1/2 cup sliced black olives
1 cup chopped pecans

Sauté the onion in the oil in a medium skillet
over medium heat until tender. Add the salsa.
Drain the spinach, squeezing out the excess
moisture. Add the spinach to the skillet. Cook
for 2 minutes, stirring frequently. Remove to a
mixing bowl. Add 2 cups of the Monterey Jack
cheese, the cream cheese, light cream and
olives and mix well. Pour into a 1 1/2-quart
baking dish. Sprinkle with the pecans. Bake,
uncovered, at 350 degrees for 15 minutes.
Cover with foil and bake for 15 minutes
longer. Sprinkle with the remaining Monterey
Jack cheese. Serve hot.

*Yield: 5 cups*

# Creamed Chicken Magnolia

*This is also an excellent luncheon entrée served in puff pastry shells or over corn bread. It would serve 12.*

3 tablespoons butter
7 tablespoons flour
2 cups warm chicken broth
2 cups warm light cream or
  milk
Salt and black pepper
  to taste
1 teaspoon dry mustard
1 teaspoon seasoned salt
1/2 teaspoon paprika
1/4 teaspoon nutmeg
1/8 teaspoon sugar
1/8 teaspoon cayenne pepper
4 hard-cooked eggs, chopped
4 cups (about) chopped
  cooked chicken
1 (8-ounce) can sliced water
  chestnuts, drained
1/4 cup madeira or sherry

Melt the butter in a saucepan over medium heat. Blend in the flour until smooth. Add the broth and cream gradually, stirring constantly until smooth. Cook until thickened, stirring constantly. Add salt and black pepper to taste, dry mustard, seasoned salt, paprika, nutmeg, sugar and cayenne pepper and mix well. Cook for 1 to 2 minutes, stirring constantly. Pour into the top of a large double boiler set over hot water. Fold in the eggs, chicken, water chestnuts and wine and mix gently. You may add 1 pound sliced fresh mushrooms sautéed in butter or canned mushrooms, drained and sautéed. Keep warm until serving time. Pour into a large chafing dish. May serve chicken in patty shells for a luncheon. Serve in Chou Puffs (page 142) or with Toast Points (below).

*Yield: 100 cocktail buffet servings*

*Cook a 5- to 6-pound hen or small turkey the day before using. Cut the meat into 1-inch pieces, pour about 1 cup or more of chicken broth over it to retain moisture, and chill, covered, until ready to use.*

# Toast Points

50 slices white bread

Remove crusts from bread. Cut each bread slice in half on the diagonal. To toast, heat oven to 250 degrees. Arrange triangles on baking sheets. Bake, turning once, for 30 minutes or until triangles are dry and toasted. Cool. Store in airtight container in refrigerator for up to 1 week or freeze for up to 3 months.

*Yield: 100 toast points*

*To Dos & Tah Dahs*

# Country Ham Cheesecake

6 tablespoons butter, melted
3 cups soup-and-oyster
  crackers, finely ground
1 cup freshly grated
  Parmesan cheese
  (about 3 ounces)
32 ounces cream cheese,
  softened
7 eggs
2 cups (8 ounces) shredded
  Swiss cheese
1 cup (1/2-inch-cubes)
  cooked country ham
1/3 cup chopped fresh chives
1 teaspoon salt
1/4 teaspoon ground white
  pepper

Brush a 9-inch springform pan with
1 tablespoon of the melted butter. Combine
the cracker crumbs, Parmesan cheese and
remaining melted butter in a bowl and mix
well. Reserve 1/2 cup of the mixture. Press the
remaining mixture over the bottom and up the
side of the prepared pan. Chill, covered, until
ready to fill. Beat the cream cheese and eggs
in a mixing bowl until smooth. Add the Swiss
cheese, ham, chives, salt and white pepper
and mix well. Pour into the prepared pan.
Sprinkle evenly with the reserved crumb
mixture. Place on a rimmed baking sheet.
Bake at 300 degrees for 2 hours or until the
filling is set and no longer moves in the center
when the pan is gently shaken. Cool in the pan
for 30 minutes. Release and remove the side of
the pan. Serve warm or at room temperature.

*Yield: 8 to 10 servings*

# Warm Brie with Caramelized Apples

1/4 cup (1/2 stick) unsalted
   butter
4 large Golden Delicious
   apples, peeled, cored,
   sliced
1/4 cup sugar
1 (12-inch) wheel Brie
   cheese
1 1/2 cup sliced almonds,
   toasted

Melt the butter in a heavy skillet over medium-
high heat. Sauté the apples in the butter for
3 minutes. Sprinkle with the sugar. Cook for
8 to 10 minutes or just until golden brown
and tender, stirring frequently. Slice the cheese
wheel in half horizontally. Spread 1/2 of the
apple mixture over the bottom 1/2 of the cheese
wheel. Top with the remaining 1/2 of the cheese
wheel. Spread the remaining apple mixture
over the top. Place on a cardboard round.
Microwave for 25 seconds on High. Place
round and all on serving tray. Top with the
almonds. Serve with Bremner Wafers.

*Yield: 50 appetizer servings*

# Artichoke Squares

2 (6-ounce) jars marinated
   artichoke hearts
1 small onion, finely
   chopped
1 garlic clove, minced
4 eggs, beaten
1/4 cup fine bread crumbs
1/2 teaspoon salt
1/4 teaspoon pepper
1/4 teaspoon oregano
1/4 teaspoon Tabasco sauce
8 ounces sharp Cheddar
   cheese, shredded (2 cups)
2 teaspoons minced fresh
   parsley

Drain the artichokes, reserving 1/2 of the
liquid. Chop the artichokes. Sauté the onion
and garlic in the reserved liquid in a skillet for
5 minutes. Combine the eggs, bread crumbs,
salt, pepper, oregano and Tabasco sauce in a
bowl and mix well. Stir in the cheese, parsley,
artichokes and onion mixture. Spoon into
a greased 7×11-inch baking dish. Bake at
325 degrees for 30 minutes or until set.
Cool in the dish for 2 hours. Cut into 1-inch
squares. Serve cold or reheat.

*Yield: 6 dozen small squares*

# Black-Eyed Pea Relish

2 (15-ounce) cans black-eyed
   peas, rinsed, drained
2 scallions, cut into 1/2-inch
   pieces
1 red bell pepper, seeded,
   finely chopped
1/2 green bell pepper, seeded,
   finely chopped (optional)
1/4 cup chopped fresh Italian
   flat-leaf parsley
1/4 cup finely chopped fresh
   chervil (optional)
1 garlic clove, minced
1/2 cup olive oil
3 tablespoons red wine
   vinegar
1 to 2 tablespoons
   whole-grain mustard
1 fresh jalapeño chile,
   seeded, minced
Salt and pepper

Combine the black-eyed peas, scallions, bell
peppers, parsley, chervil and garlic in a large
salad bowl and toss to mix. Combine the olive
oil, vinegar, whole-grain mustard, jalapeño
chile, salt and pepper in a small bowl and whisk
until blended. Pour over the black-eyed pea
mixture and toss to coat. Serve or refrigerate.
Serve with pita chips.

*Yield: 30 servings*

# Caviar Eggs

10 medium eggs, chilled
2 teaspoons salt
1/3 cup sour cream
3 tablespoons minced onion
2 teaspoons lemon juice
1 teaspoon grated lemon zest
2 tablespoons caviar
40 (3/4-inch long) chive tips

Combine the eggs and 1 teaspoon of the salt
in water to cover in a saucepan. Bring to a
boil over high heat. Boil for 10 minutes.
Remove from the heat. Let stand, covered, for
20 minutes. Drain and cover with cold water.
Peel and cut the eggs in half lengthwise. Mash
the yolks in a bowl until creamy. Add the sour
cream, onion, lemon juice, lemon zest and
remaining salt and mix until creamy. Stuff the
egg whites evenly with the yolk mixture. Top
each egg half with 1/4 teaspoon of the caviar
and 2 chive tips.

*Yield: 20 servings*

# Pork Tenderloin with Mustard Caper Sauce

1¹/2 cups mayonnaise
¹/2 cup sour cream
1 small jar capers, drained
3 tablespoons white wine
2 tablespoons Dijon mustard
¹/2 teaspoon white pepper
2 to 3 pounds pork
    tenderloin
1 jar honey-cup mustard

Combine the mayonnaise, sour cream, capers, wine, Dijon mustard and white pepper in a bowl and mix well. Chill, covered, in the refrigerator. Rinse the pork and pat dry with paper towels. Place the pork on a rack in a roasting pan. Roast at 325 degrees for 30 minutes. Spread 1 cup of the honey-cup mustard over the pork. Roast for 30 minutes more until the pork is cooked through and reaches an internal temperature of 170 degrees on a meat thermometer. Serve the pork on the Sweet Potato Biscuits with the mustard sauce.

*Yield: 30 servings*

# Sweet Potato Biscuits

2 to 3 medium sweet
    potatoes, peeled, cut into
    1-inch cubes
¹/2 cup (1 stick) butter
¹/2 cup sugar
1 teaspoon salt
3¹/2 to 4 cups flour
4¹/2 teaspoons baking
    powder
¹/2 teaspoon cinnamon

Boil the sweet potatoes in water to cover in a saucepan until tender; drain. Mash the sweet potatoes. Measure 1¹/2 cups of the mashed potatoes and place in a large bowl. Reserve any remaining mashed potatoes for another use. Add the butter, sugar and salt to the potatoes and mix well. Sift 3¹/2 cups of the flour, the baking powder and cinnamon together. Add to the potato mixture and mix well. Knead the mixture, adding the remaining flour, if necessary, to make a soft dough. Wrap the dough in plastic wrap and chill for 30 minutes or longer. Roll the dough ¹/2 inch thick and cut into rounds using a 2¹/2-inch biscuit cutter. Arrange on a greased baking sheet. Bake at 350 degrees for 15 minutes or until the biscuits begin to brown. May be prepared ahead and frozen.

*Yield: 16 biscuits*

*You may substitute lite sour cream and low-fat mayonnaise for the sour cream and mayonnaise in the Mustard Caper Sauce.*

# Red Potatoes with Gorgonzola Cream, Bacon and Pecans

12 extra-small red potatoes
1 tablespoon olive oil
1/2 teaspoon coarse kosher salt
2 tablespoons minced fresh chives
Gorgonzola Cream (below)

Combine the potatoes, olive oil, kosher salt and chives in a bowl and toss to coat. Place on a baking sheet. Roast at 400 degrees for 45 minutes or until the potatoes are tender. Cool slightly. Scoop out 1 teaspoon of flesh from each potato and fill with Gorgonzola Cream, or slice the potatoes and top each slice with Gorgonzola Cream. Garnish with additional minced fresh chives.

*Yield: 24 servings*

## Gorgonzola Cream

*Slices of red potatoes could be used instead of the whole potatoes. Potatoes could be simmered until tender in water (instead of roasting), cooled, and sliced.*

8 ounces cream cheese, softened
1/4 cup (about 3 ounces) Gorgonzola cheese, softened
1/2 teaspoon freshly ground pepper
1/4 teaspoon hot pepper sauce
6 slices bacon, crisp-cooked, finely crumbled
1/4 cup pecan halves, toasted, finely chopped
Whipping cream

Combine the cream cheese, Gorgonzola cheese, pepper, hot pepper sauce, bacon and pecans in a bowl and mix well. Stir in enough whipping cream to make of the desired consistency. Chill, covered, until serving time. May prepare 1 day ahead.

# Devil's Fudge

*The combination of chocolate and peanuts is wonderful.*
*Liz Pilgrim shared this recipe.*

2 cups sugar
3/4 cup evaporated milk
2 tablespoons margarine
1 cup (6 ounces) semisweet
   chocolate chips
1 teaspoon vanilla extract
1 cup salted cocktail peanuts

Combine the sugar, evaporated milk and margarine in a saucepan and mix well. Bring to a full boil, stirring constantly. Boil for 3 minutes, stirring constantly. Remove from the heat. Add the chocolate chips and stir until melted and smooth. Stir in the vanilla and peanuts. Spread in a lightly greased 8×8-inch baking pan. Chill until firm.

*Yield: 10 to 12 servings*

# A Guide for a Cocktail Party for 30

*1 bottle rum or tequila*
*2 bottles gin*
*3 bottles vodka*
*1 bottle Scotch*
*1 bottle bourbon*
*9 bottles white wine (Chardonnary, Chalbis, or Vouvray)*
*6 bottles red wine (Merlot, Cabernet Sauvignon, or Pinot Noir)*
*12 bottles of beer—4 regular, 8 light*
*6 large bottles each tonic soda, cola, and diet soda*
*6 to 7 bottles mineral water*
*Lemons and limes*
*Large green olives*
*40 pounds of ice—15 for cocktails and 25 for chilling bottles*

*The vanilla bean was cultivated and processed by the Aztecs who put it into their cocoa-based drink. It is labor intensive to process, so that is why it is so expensive.*

*Pure vanilla extract is made by macerating the chopped beans in an alcohol water solution. Imitation vanilla is composed entirely of artificial flavorings, most of which are paper industry by-products.*

# A Wedding Reception

*Champagne*
*Chafing Dish Crab in Tartlet Shells • Classic Creamed Mushrooms in*
*Chou Puffs • Mexican Egg Salad in Cherry Tomatoes*
*Apricot Brandied Brie • Tiny Potatoes with Bacon and Avocado*
*Fresh Fruit with Raspberry Dip • Turkey or Ham with*
*Angel Biscuits • Wedding Cake*

Wedding receptions today seem to be both casual and formal in most parts of the country. One of the most beautiful and delicious wedding receptions that I have ever attended was Lucy Bowen Caddell's and Bruce Taylor's. Lucy is the daughter of my good friends Tom and Becki Caddell. It was held at the St. Francis Hotel in San Francisco and not a detail was missed. There were specialty stations; pasta stations, meat stations, cheese stations, dim sum stations, and a miniature dessert station. The towering cake was beautiful with layers of strawberries between each tier. Quite elegant, as was the bride. The wedding menu that we will present will be one with substantial food, following a 6:30 p.m. formal wedding. A wedding held after 6:30 p.m. or at noon, is considered very formal and is generally black tie. Let me reiterate that you may have much lighter fare at an afternoon reception following a ceremony from 2 to 4 o'clock in the afternoon. A menu of fruit and cheese, finger sandwiches, punch and cake would be very adequate. I can remember that is exactly what Bill and I had at our wedding reception years ago in Cartersville, Georgia. It was a 4:30 p.m. ceremony.

Most people hire a professional caterer since there are so many other details to arrange. If you are a caterer or a nonprofessional attempting to cater a wedding, most of the menu items may be prepared ahead. Wedding receptions may have very light food or heavier food depending on the time of day. Many items can be prepared ahead. All of these items can be done in advance if you choose not to have a caterer.

# Chafing Dish Crab

6 tablespoons butter
1/3 cup chopped scallions
3 tablespoons flour
2 1/2 cups half-and-half
4 ounces cream cheese,
    cubed
1 pound fresh or canned
    lump crab meat, drained
1/4 cup dry vermouth
Juice of 1/2 lemon
2 teaspoons Worcestershire
    sauce
Salt and white pepper

Melt the butter in a heavy saucepan. Sauté the scallions in the butter. Stir in the flour. Cook until the mixture bubbles, stirring constantly. Add the half-and-half and cook until thickened, stirring constantly. Add the cream cheese 1 cube at a time, stirring after each addition. Add the crab meat, vermouth, lemon juice, Worcestershire sauce, salt and white pepper and mix well. Spoon into baked tartlet shells and serve or serve with toast points (page 149).

*Yield: 25 appetizer servings*

# Tartlet Shells

2 1/2 cups flour
1 teaspoon salt
1 cup (2 sticks) chilled
    unsalted butter,
    sliced
5 tablespoons ice water

Combine the flour and salt in a food processor and process until mixed. Cut in the butter by pulsing several times until crumbly. Add the ice water and process until the mixture begins to form moist clumps, adding additional ice water if dough is dry. Shape into a ball. Wrap in plastic wrap and chill for 30 minutes or longer. Roll the dough 1/8 inch thick. Cut dough with a 2 1/2-inch scalloped cutter. Press into 48 miniature muffin pan cups. Pierce the dough all over with a fork; chill. Bake at 400 degrees for 14 minutes or until golden brown. Cool in the pan on a wire rack. Remove the tartlet shells from the pan carefully.

*Yield: 48 shells*

# Classic Creamed Mushrooms

1 cup (2 sticks) unsalted
  butter
1 pound wild mushrooms,
  sliced
1/4 cup sliced scallions
1/2 cup flour
11/2 cups half-and-half
1/2 cup (2 ounces) shredded
  Swiss cheese
1/3 cup sour cream
1/2 cup chopped pecans,
  toasted

Melt 1 stick butter in a skillet until tender.
Add the mushrooms and sauté until tender.
Drain and set aside. Combine the remaining
butter and the scallions in a microwave-safe
dish. Microwave, covered, for 2 minutes.
Stir in the flour. Stir in the half-and-half.
Microwave, uncovered, for 2 to 3 minutes or
until thick, stirring once every minute. Add
the cheese, stirring until melted. Add the
sour cream and mushrooms and mix well.
Microwave, uncovered, for 1 minute longer,
stirring once, halfway through the cooking
time. Sprinkle with the pecans. Serve in
pastry cups or in Chou Puff shells (page 142).

*Yield: 8 to 10 servings*

*Remember that one gallon
of punch will serve
32 people one 4-ounce cup.
If you are planning on a
late afternoon wedding
and food on the heavy
side, have between 8 to
10 items. If you are
serving Champagne, there
are 12 bottles to a case or
approximately 75 flute
glasses of 4 to 5 ounces.*

# Angel Biscuits

*Angel Biscuits are delicious sliced while still warm and spread with an herb or fruit-flavored butter and filled with thin slices of country ham, smoked turkey, or smoked salmon. Purchase some wonderful sun-dried tomato bread, dillweed bread, or walnut bread and slice very thinly for the meat toppings. These breads can be found at most bakeries.*

2 envelopes dry yeast
$1/4$ cup warm water
5 cups flour
1 tablespoon baking powder
1 teaspoon baking soda
$2^1/2$ tablespoons sugar
1 teaspoon salt
1 cup (2 sticks) unsalted
  butter, cut into small
  pieces
2 cups buttermilk
$1/2$ cup (1 stick) unsalted
  butter, melted, cooled

Dissolve the yeast in the water in a small bowl and allow to proof. Sift the flour, baking powder, baking soda, sugar and salt into a large bowl. Cut in 1 cup butter until the mixture resembles coarse meal. Stir in the yeast mixture and buttermilk. Knead the dough on a floured surface until smooth and no longer sticky. Roll $1/2$ inch thick and cut out $1^1/2$-inch rounds with a biscuit cutter. Arrange 2 inches apart on a buttered or parchment paper-lined baking sheet. Brush the tops with $1/2$ cup melted butter. Bake at 450 degrees for 10 to 12 minutes or until light golden but not brown. Serve with ham or turkey.

*Yield: 48 biscuits*

# Apricot Brandied Brie

*This is a sophisticated appetizer prepared in just minutes.*

1 (1-pound) wheel imported
　Brie cheese, rind removed
Lemon leaves or fig leaves
1 cup apricot preserves
1/2 cup mandarin Napoleon
　brandy or Cognac
2 French baguettes, sliced
　1/2 inch thick, toasted

Let the cheese stand at room temperature for 1 hour. Pierce in several places with a fork. Arrange the lemon leaves on a platter and place the cheese on top. Combine the apricot preserves and brandy in a medium saucepan and mix well. Heat until hot but not boiling. Pour over the cheese. Garnish with strawberries and/or grapes. Serve with the baguette slices or Crostini (page 117).

*Yield: variable*

# Tiny Potatoes
# with Bacon and Avocado

12 tiny red potatoes
1 pound bacon, cut into
　1-inch pieces
1 cup sour cream
1/4 cup chopped cilantro
1 avocado, chopped
1 large tomato, chopped

Scrub the potatoes and pierce in several places with a fork or knife. Place in a baking pan. Bake at 425 degrees for 40 minutes or until tender. Let stand to cool. Cut the potatoes into halves and scoop out the centers with a spoon or melon baller, leaving a 1/4-inch-thick shell. Set aside. Reserve the scooped out centers for another use. Cook the bacon in a skillet until crisp. Drain on paper towels. Combine the bacon, sour cream, cilantro, avocado and tomato in a bowl and mix well. Fill the potato shells with the bacon mixture. Serve warm or at room temperature.

*Yield: 24 appetizer servings*

# Mexican Egg Salad

*Fill cherry tomatoes (hollowed out and drained) with this salad and serve on a bed of Belgian endive on a fancy tray, or mound the salad on a serving tray and serve with crackers. The salad also makes a great sandwich filling.*

12 hard-cooked eggs, grated
1¹/2 cups (6 ounces)
   shredded sharp Cheddar
   cheese
4 ribs celery, finely chopped
5 scallions, sliced
2 fresh jalapeño chiles,
   minced
1 red bell pepper, finely
   chopped
1 garlic clove, minced
1 cup mayonnaise
Juice of 1 lime
1 tablespoon cumin
1 tablespoon chili powder
Salt and pepper

Combine the eggs, cheese, celery, scallions, jalapeño chiles, bell pepper and garlic in a large bowl and mix well. Combine the mayonnaise, lime juice, cumin, chili powder, salt and pepper in a small bowl and whisk until blended. Pour over the egg mixture and mix well, adding additional mayonnaise if necessary to make of the desired consistency. Chill, covered, until serving time. Garnish with coriander and avocado.

*Yield: 6 to 8 servings*

# Fresh Fruit with Raspberry Dip

24 ounces cream cheese,
   softened
¹/2 cup red raspberry
   preserves
1 cup heavy cream
2 teaspoons vanilla extract
Fresh pineapple chunks
Fresh cantaloupe chunks
Fresh honeydew melon
   chunks
Kiwifruit slices
Navel orange slices
Star fruit slices
Fresh strawberries

Beat the cream cheese in a mixing bowl until smooth and creamy. Add the raspberry preserves, cream and vanilla and beat until well blended. Spoon into a serving bowl and place in the center of a platter. Arrange the pineapple, cantaloupe, honeydew melon, kiwifruit, oranges, star fruit and strawberries on the platter surrounding the dip.

*Yield: variable*

# Appendix

# Decorating Ideas

For a simple centerpiece, try one of the following ideas:

- Trim the stems of half a dozen tulips so that the petals barely reach the rim of a clear glass vase. Fill the vase with water so that the blooms are below water level.

- Arrange a few sugared pears and a sugared grape cluster in a shallow bowl. To sugar the fruit, dip it into lightly beaten egg whites, roll it lightly in a bowl of granulated sugar, and set it on towels to dry for several hours.

- Fill three similarly shaped vases of various heights with three different flower types. For example, place freesias in one vase, irises in another, and daffodils or hyacinths in a third. Place the vases on the table in an attractive grouping.

- Wrap a large hosta leaf or banana leaf around the inside surface of a glass vase. Fill the vase with water so that the leaf is submerged. Set blossoming quince or apple branches in the vase.

- Make a daisy chain, or simply arrange daisies in an interlocking fashion, and place the flowers lengthwise along the center of the table.

For an easy bouquet:

Unlike sticking flower stems in a wire holder or florist foam, or jamming them in a vase, a bouquet made in the hand is easily adjusted until the arrangement is perfect and ready to tie together. First, strip or cut away the lower leaves. Take three stems. Hold at the center of their length and fan out the tops so that the flowers are evenly spaced. Continue adding more stems, one at a time, until a spiraling formation becomes apparent, with each bloom arranged to show its best side. When the bouquet is evenly rounded, tie raffia several times around the stems at the juncture where the hand has held them in place. Place in a vase of water.

# Entertaining Tips

- Plan the date, time, place, budget, and duration of the party.
- Plan a menu that can be easily executed by you.
- Shop early.
- Do as much advance preparation as possible.
- Calculate how much to buy.
- Be flexible when developing your menu.
- Set the table, make centerpieces, and be sure linens are pressed.
- Make a work plan and timetable.
- Leave plenty of time to prepare yourself.
- Delegate some chores to others.
- Have all china in place.
- Have the sink filled with soapy water to ease the burden of cleaning.
- Plan a short workout to help you to be relaxed and cheerful.
- Serve at a leisurely pace.
- If you are not an experienced entertainer then keep it simple.

# Getting Organized for a Party

- Don't take anything for granted.
- Send out invitations 2 to 3 weeks in advance of the party. People get busy during the holidays.
- Make sure the room is cool before the party starts, even in winter.
- Move big, cumbersome furniture out of the way along with anything fragile.
- Set up the bar away from the entrance if possible and allow for plenty of room in front and to the sides of it. Never put a bar or food table at the end of a long room or in a place where there is only one way in or out. This will eliminate bottlenecks.
- Cover the bar with a floor-length cloth so you can store extra glasses and what-not out of the way under it.
- Introduce guests to each other.
- Start serving hot hors d'oeuvre when 8 or so guests have arrived.
- Replace hot hors d'oeuvre frequently.
- You can rent almost anything you don't have.
- Make sure you see what you are renting before you order it.
- Don't forget about a place to put coats. If your bed won't do the trick, rent coat racks.

# Planning an Appetizer Buffet

The caterer's rule of thumb on beverages is 1 to $1^1/2$ drinks per hour per guest. If you're in a quandary about how much to buy, ask your beverage store if you can return any unopened bottles. It has been noted that people are drinking less alcohol now, so you'll likely need more wine, bottled waters, and soft drinks than you may expect and less hard liquor.

A bar with wine, beer, and mineral water is adequate for most groups. Keep food and beverage tables separated for traffic flow.

Time has a lot to do with planning. Some caterers suggest for a two-hour party, a minimum of 12 finger food pieces per guest—ten pieces of hors d'oeuvre and two sweets. Allow two shrimp per person if it is served. It is very popular.

If a party is to start at 7:00 p.m., it must serve as dinner. We figure 21 bites per person. If the party starts at 8:30 p.m. or later, go light on savories and offer more sweets. Know your guests. Young people eat more than an older crowd. Guests eat more at casual parties.

# How Much for How Many

For 50 guests you will need 1 bartender. The following amounts are for 20-guest and 50-guest parties. You may choose to have more or less of some items depending on your menu.

| Wines | 20-Guest Party | 50-Guest Party |
|---|---|---|
| Champagne | 3 bottles | 6 to 7 bottles |
| White Wine | 3 to 4 bottles | 6 to 8 bottles |
| Red Wine | 4 to 5 bottles | 11 to 12 bottles |
| Sparkling Water or Mineral Water | 12 (10-ounce) bottles | 24 (10-ounce) bottle |

Wine: These estimates are based on consumption of two or three (4-ounce) glasses per person over a three-hour period with food.

Chill all white wine and Champagne for at least three hours before guests arrive. Open about two bottles of red wine 30 minutes before guests arrive. Open additional wine as needed.

# Flowers Edible and Toxic

There has been a recent awakening in awareness of the delicious possibilities from the garden. Here are some of my favorite edible flowers:

| | | | |
|---|---|---|---|
| Anise hyssop | Chive | English lavender | Pansy |
| Bay laurel | Daylily | Marigold | Rose |
| Bee balm | Dandelion | Mustard | Rosemary |
| Borage | Scented geranium | Nasturtium | Winter savory |
| Chamomile | Hollyhock | Marjoram | |

Use them in salads to add color and surprising flavor. Or try them as a substitute for lettuce in sandwiches. Experiment with them in many ways until you find the best complements for their sometimes unusual flavors.

Always remember that some flowers and plants are poisonous when consumed, and you should be careful when experimenting with them. Here is a list of the most common garden plants that are harmful. However, check every type of plant before you serve it to your guests or eat it yourself.

| | | |
|---|---|---|
| Bleeding heart | Foxglove | Periwinkle |
| Daffodil | Hydrangea | Poinsettia |
| Delphinium | Monkshood | Primrose |
| | Oleander | |

# *Index*

# Index

# Index

# Index

# Index

# Index

# To order additional copies of

## *Southern Scrumptious Entertains*

write to:

*Scrumptious, Inc.*
4107 Indian Hills Road
Decatur, Alabama 35603
Visit our website at www.scrumptiousinc.com

Be sure to include Your Name and Complete Address for return mail.

| | |
|---|---|
| For one copy of *Southern Scrumptious Entertains* send: | $21.95 |
| Plus sales tax | 1.98 |
| Plus postage and handling | 3.00 |
| Total | $26.93 |

| | |
|---|---|
| For one copy of *Southern Scrumptious How to Cater Your Own Party* send: | $19.95 |
| Plus sales tax | 1.80 |
| Plus postage and handling | 3.00 |
| Total | $24.75 |

[  ]  Desire gift wrap.

For volume purchases call 1-256-353-1897 or email mettysims@aol.com.

Make checks payable to *Scrumptious, Inc.*

[  ] VISA     [  ] MasterCard     Exp. Date _____

Account Number _____

Signature _____

# About the Author

Betty Brandon Sims majored in Foods and Nutrition at the University of Tennessee. A member of the International Association of Cooking Professionals, she has edited several regional cookbooks and is the author of *Southern Scrumptious, How to Cater Your Own Party*. She has studied at many prestigious cooking schools at home and abroad.

Betty has long been active in her community and in the food business, having previously owned Johnston Street Cafe and a very busy catering business. At present, she owns Scrumptious, Inc., a food business specializing in speaking, writing, and cooking classes.

Mrs. Sims lives in Decatur, Alabama, with her husband, Dr. Bill Sims. Her family includes Libby Sims Patrick, Carl, and Alex; Sheri Sims Hofherr, Brandon, and Finlay; Bill Sims, Jr., Tara, Will, and Allison; Lisa Sims Wallace, Paul, Paul Jr., and Sims.